THE FOUR IMMEASURABLES

THE FOUR IMMEASURABLES

Practices to Open the Heart

B. Alan Wallace

Edited by
Zara Houshmand

Snow Lion
Boulder

Snow Lion
An imprint of Shambhala Publications, Inc.
4720 Walnut Street
Boulder, Colorado 80301
www.shambhala.com

This book was originally published under the title *Boundless Heart: The Four Immeasurables.*

14 13 12 11 10 9 8 7 6

Printed in the United States of America

⊗ This edition is printed on acid-free paper that meets the American National Standards Institute Z39.48 Standard.
♻ Shambhala Publications makes every effort to print on recycled paper. For more information please visit www.shambhala.com.
Snow Lion is distributed worldwide by Penguin Random House, Inc., and its subsidiaries.

The Library of Congress catalogues the previous edition of this book as follows:
Wallace, B. Alan.
Boundless heart: the four immeasurables / by B. Alan Wallace; edited by Zara Houshmand.
p. cm.
ISBN 978-1-55939-119-1 (1st edition)
ISBN 978-1-55939-209-9 (2nd edition)
ISBN 978-1-55939-353-9 (3rd edition)
1. Meditation—Buddhism. 2. Spiritual life—Buddhism. 3. Buddhism—China—Tibet—Doctrines. I. Houshmand, Zara. II. Title.
BQ5612.W35 1999
294.3'444—dc21
99-31831
CIP

Contents

Preface

The teachings presented in this book took shape during a one-week retreat led by Alan Wallace for a small group of friends in the summer of 1992, above the town of Lone Pine in the Eastern Sierra Nevada Mountains. The informal talks that Alan gave were based in part on passages from Buddhaghosa's fifth-century compendium called The *Path of Purification*, though his interpretations were clearly influenced by his training in Tibetan Buddhism. The passages in question related to the cultivation of *śamatha* (pronounced "sha-ma-ta"), or meditative quiescence as it is sometimes known, and the Four Immeasurables (*catvāryapramāṇi*): loving-kindness, compassion, empathetic joy, and equanimity. These practices, of *śamatha* and the Four Immeasurables, are very different but profoundly complementary: they enrich, deepen, and protect each other. Also included are guided meditations that Alan led, and portions of the very lively and wide-ranging group discussions that took place.

Chapter One
Introduction

WHY PRACTICE?

Buddhist practice starts not with a leap of faith, but with a careful observation of our own experience. Among the many facets of experience that we can attend to, Buddhism pays special attention to the phenomenon of suffering: the first Noble Truth. It is a good place to start and it grabs our attention. Most of us can relate to the observation that there is suffering.

The very fertile question is, why? What makes us prone to suffering? If I fall off my bike and scrape my knee, and then ask why I'm suffering, it's a fairly trivial question. But if I am sitting here in one of the most beautiful places on the planet, healthy, with a full belly, and still I'm unhappy, then the question becomes very interesting. What's going on? Why should unhappiness arise? Why is there suffering of the mind? The question also becomes interesting when disharmony and conflict arise in relationships with other people. What causes the suffering of interpersonal conflict or international conflict? Why can't we just get along? It's another way of asking the second Noble Truth: What is the source of suffering?

Although there are myriad conditions that give rise to conflict and internal distress, many of the external factors are not really essential to the suffering that we experience. This is not to devalue the external factors, but the internal factors are more essential. And though many external factors are beyond our control, the internal factors happily offer more possibility for transmutation.

What is essential to this suffering? What is invariably present as a source of the suffering we experience? As the Buddha was pursuing these questions, he drew the conclusion from his own experience that certain fundamental afflictions of the mind are the source of the distress we experience, whether in solitude, or in our relationships with other people and the environment. The most fundamental of these afflictions is delusion. We are actively misconstruing reality, and that messes things up. From this active misconstruction of reality arise other distortions of the mind. The Sanskrit word for mental affliction is *kleśa*. It is related to the word *kliṣṭa*, which means to twist or to be warped. As we look out on the world through the window of our mind, somehow the window gets warped. What we are seeing is reality, but a twisted reality, and we respond to it in an unstraightforward way. The Tibetan word for an adept, or highly realized being (*drang srong*) means straight, not twisted.

The fundamental problem is delusion. As Jesus said, "Father, forgive them, for they do not know what they are doing." [1] He put his finger right on the button: The crucial problem is that we don't know what we're doing. And from this delusion, other twistings of the mind occur: selfish craving, hostility, aggression, and a myriad other derivative afflictions.

Is it possible to be free of these sources of suffering, or are they simply part and parcel of being human? Is it possible to be free of them, not by repressing them or by taking a vacation or respite from them, but by totally, irrevocably eradicating these internal sources of affliction? It is an extraordinary question, a question the Buddha pursued for years. And from his own experience he drew the conclusion: Yes, it is possible. And so we engage with the four Noble Truths: suffering, the source of suffering, liberation from the source of suffering, and finally, the path to that liberation. Thereon hangs the rest of the tale.

If the root problem is delusion, then the root antidote must be something that meets that delusion head on. The root antidote for delusion is probably not loving-kindness. Loving-kindness can serve as the antidote for hatred, indifference, or self-centeredness, but the root antidote for delusion is the realization of insight. Of the two wings of enlightenment, compassion and wisdom, the wisdom of insight is the one that meets delusion head on. This is why Buddhist practice places so much emphasis on the cultivation of insight (*vipaśyanā*).

Delusion takes various forms, but key to them all is an illusion concerning our own existence—who we are. A fruitful hypothesis (not dogma that we must believe) is that we are falsely construing ourselves as something existing independently, autonomously, separately from the environment and from other sentient beings. This little ego struggles through life, reaching for all good things and pushing all bad things away. Insofar as we buy into this false construction of reality, then implicitly we have already bound ourselves to conflict. If I—the independent, autonomous Alan—approach another person, I do so not as a static rock, but with a lot of desires concerning my own well-being and the fulfillment of my happiness. And if the person whom I approach has a similar program, we have a conflict right from the start. If there is a whole room full of people, the problem increases proportionately.

We would be happier without that delusion, and insight is a way to cut right through it. It doesn't happen through faith in any dogma or belief system, but it is something we can know experientially without any shadow of a doubt. Insight is a mode of experience that cuts through the delusion incompatible with that experience, and the cutting edge of Buddhist practice in meditation is the cultivation of insight. What kind of insight? The emphasis is on realizing the nature of self. If we don't exist in autonomous, self-sufficient isolation, then how do we exist? And how can this become more than simply a philosophical conclusion? How does it become an insight?

We cultivate the insight through a very close inquiry into the nature of our own being and experience. Mindfulness is essential here. This careful exploration leads to a vivid, un-mediated experience of phenomena: of our own mental states, our feelings and desires, our perception of our body and the environment. It leads to a realization that this "I" we have been clinging to for so long doesn't exist at all. It's not that we do not exist—that would be a silly conclusion—but that this particular "I" that we sense as separate and autonomous is simply nonexistent. This little ego does not exist: the one that tries to be in charge and has a real hard time, the one that gets so fearful and tries to plug down its emotions. The sense of it definitely exists, most grossly when we feel egotistical or ar-rogant, but this sense has no more referent than if I truly be-lieved I were Napoleon and expected everyone to salute me as such. The sense we have of our own selves is just as de-luded, because there is no referent. The idea is to inquire care-fully into our own experience, our own will, mental states, feelings, past history, future desires, our whole sense of who we are—and see for ourselves whether there is any substan-tial referent to this sense of "I." And if we do realize that no such self exists, where are we then?

There is a story told of Tsongkhapa, who lived in fifteenth-century Tibet. He was teaching to a group of monks about just this understanding of the emptiness of ego, and among this group was a monk from the district of Narthang who was listening very attentively. Sometimes, if there is a certain rap-port between teacher and student, it's possible that just hear-ing the words can have a very great power for transforma-tion. Tsongkhapa was just homing in on his point, that the self as we sense it does not exist, when the monk suddenly grabbed his collar as if he'd been hit by a jolt of electricity.

Tsongkhapa saw this gesture, picked the man out from the crowd, and said, "Aha, this fellow from Narthang has just established his conventional self on the basis of his collar." The story may date from the fifteenth century, but what happened to the monk is neither ancient history nor very exceptional. It is not uncommon, when you start meditating, to experience a sudden sense of disorientation that makes you grab for something to hold on to. This fellow found his collar. I remember a person who was meditating very earnestly and intently, under the guidance of quite a realized teacher, and had a very profound realization with a radical shift of experience. It scared the living daylights out of this individual, and the experience then became something that had to be repressed. We have enough trauma in our lives without seeking out spiritual experiences that we then need to repress.

When you perceive your very self as identityless—as an experience and not just as a philosophical position—this realization can come as the most precious of all possible treasures, utterly transformative and beyond compare. Or instead, you may perceive it as a loss of the greatest of all possible treasures. To meditate arduously only to find that you have lost your most treasured possession—your self—seems like time not very well spent. The difference in these two experiences is really a fork in the road, a sheep-and-goats division; and the difference depends on the context in which you perceive the realization. Some groundwork is needed to ensure that you can welcome and embrace deep insight when it occurs, so that it enriches your life rather than giving you a sense of existential impoverishment. We can help ourselves to move toward the more fruitful of these two directions by gradually loosening our grip on our separate and autonomous sense of "I," not just intellectually but in our emotional lives and the choices we make.

It also helps to develop a sense of ourselves in relationship to others. I am my parent's child, I am a spouse, I am a teacher, I am a student, I am in a community, I am interrelated. The patchwork quilt of who we are derives from many sources: what others have told us, how people respond to us, how we relate to solitude. Our very sense of who we are is itself a dependently related event. It is fairly easy to understand cerebrally that we exist in relation to others, but as we lead our lives and follow our aspirations, are we doing so as if our own well-being were totally unrelated to that of anyone else? If so, then we are living a fraud and our hearts don't know what our minds are saying. As we start to live with the sense not only that we exist in interrelationship, but that our very well-being exists only in relationship to other people, then "*my* well-being" simply becomes a mere convention. Insofar as this becomes real and not just an assertion, then our grip on our autonomous ego softens. And insofar as we take into account the well-being of others, their sorrows and joys, and the fact that every sentient being wishes for happiness just as we do—insofar as we start to live this, it becomes our reality. As William James said, "our belief and attention are the same fact. For the moment, what we attend to is reality...."[2] The previous reality of "my" desires, "my" joys and sorrows, doesn't get snuffed. Rather, it becomes part of the larger family. It takes on a broader context.

Imagine really embodying this quality of attending carefully from the heart and mind to the well-being of others, even as we continue to attend to our own. This is not self-negation, but rather self-contextualization. Imagine living life as if we already knew that we exist in interrelationship, with this norm as a platform from which to seek a realization of the absence of our autonomous, controlling ego. The realization then becomes an affirmation of our way of life. The chances become better and better that the realization will entail finding the greatest treasure and not losing it.

There is another reason, too, for laying a strong foundation. In practicing any meditation designed to yield radically transforming insight, whether in the Vipassanā, Zen, or Tibetan Buddhist traditions, it is possible to get tantalizing glimmers that drift away elusively. It's like smelling something wonderful cooking in the next room. You try to track it down, but you hardly catch a little taste before it flits off, because the mind is not stable enough to enter into the insight and rest in it. Again, some groundwork is needed before we can sustain our realizations so they are not reduced to mere episodes in memory. So many people have an experience of tremendous value, but they cannot get access to it again. A year goes by, ten years, twenty years; it fades. It's better than if it had never happened, but if it was worthwhile at all, how much better to enter into it repeatedly, deepen it, and let it saturate your experience.

If we want to enter into very deep realization and new modes of experience, we should be well equipped to do so with stability and continuity. Insofar as we can do this, the realization has the greatest possibility of saturating our experience, our beliefs, our emotions. If we can abide in such realization with continuity and clarity, it will be radically transformative. Otherwise it's merely a flirtation.

That is the reason, from the top down, why we would want to cultivate both quiescence and the Four Immeasurables. The cultivation of quiescence and the Four Immeasurables lays a foundation so that the experience of insight will be favorable, with a deeply transformative value. Insight practice alone might be adequate if we were living in complete isolation from the environment, but that is not true. We are already embodied as full participants in life, with all of its tremendous diversity and its vicissitudes. It is possible to do a meditation retreat with great sincerity, earnestness, and determination; to develop some degree of stability and vividness; and then coming from that experience, to engage with people once again with conflict and hostility, completely blowing away everything you have accomplished. All that effort is shattered with one burst of anger, let alone the machine-gun bursts of repeated anger, craving, and jealousy.

For better or worse, our spiritual practice takes place within the context of our life; and for better or worse, our life entails a lot more than formal spiritual practice. It entails having children, spouses, parents, jobs. The quality of our behavior can be very destructive, unraveling any progress we have made in our formal spiritual practice. The bedrock of our practice does not lie in any meditation technique; the bedrock is our lives. The quality of how we spend our waking, and even our sleeping hours needs to be a fertile ground, so that once we start to grow and mature in our practice, the roots can go deeper and the sprout can come to fruition.

THE FOUNDATION OF ETHICS

This approach to Buddhist practice is a three-tiered pyramid, with insight at the apex as the cutting edge. The second tier, which facilitates insight and makes it effective, is meditation practice, including quiescence and the Four Immeasurables. The first tier at ground level is ethical discipline: turning our way of life into a fertile ground for our other practices. We don't need to be perfect saints to make progress; that would be a Catch-22 situation, obviously. But there are some guidelines that can protect us.

It's so frustrating to invest time in your practice only to have it shattered. Tibetans have been joking about this for so long, sometimes laughing at themselves and sometimes at us. They have met truckloads of earnest Westerners coming to India and Nepal, or to Buddhist centers in this country, striving so diligently in meditation retreats. The Tibetans say it is as if they come in for a shower, bathe clean, then jump in the nearest mudhole and wallow in it. Then they rush back to the shower, into retreat again, then back to the goop in the mudhole, back and forth, again and again. They think it's funny because it doesn't work.

Spiritual practice, which is intended to remove suffering and to lead us to experience the glorious potential of the human spirit, is like the sprout of a little tree. When it's still very small, even a baby rabbit could come along and decapitate it. End of story. One future tree just bit the dust. You build a fence around it so the rabbits can't get to it. Later you may have to put up larger fences for the deer or the elephants. You build whatever fences you need to protect something that is terribly vulnerable and extraordinarily precious—your happiness. Ethical discipline is really a way of protecting yourself so that your efforts in spiritual practice can flourish without getting stomped to smithereens every other day, or every other year.

The guidelines are fairly simple. If you only want one, instead of the 253 precepts that a monk takes on, avoid inflicting injury on yourself or others. We could stop right there. If you are imaginative, you can extrapolate all 253 from that one. There are ten, however, that are enormously helpful in a general way. The first three pertain to the physical body. Then there are four for speech, because we use speech an awful lot. And finally, three relate to the mind. Bear in mind that they are all a protection for your own well-being, in solitude or in community.

1. Avoiding killing, as far as possible. It's true that if we breathe or eat, we kill. At the very least, bacteria are getting knocked off. Being absolutely pure is an impossible notion, but we can be more pure than impure. We can inflict less killing rather than more.
2. Avoid sexual misconduct. This applies especially to adultery, but more generally to using the sexual domain as an area for inflicting injury.
3. Avoid taking what is not given.
4. Avoid lying. This is an obvious one: avoid consciously, intentionally deceiving others, leading them away from truth.
5. Avoid slander. Slander has nothing to do with whether the words are true or false. But if the motivation is to create divisions between people or provoke enmity, that's slander. If it's false, it's a lie too.
6. Avoid abuse. This has nothing to do with whether you are telling the truth or a falsehood. Speech can be completely true with no exaggeration at all, and still be entirely abuse. It has to do with motivation. Are we using our words as weapons to wound someone? If the motivation behind the words is to inflict injury, it is abuse.

7. Avoid idle gossip. This refers not to casual talk—as if we were only supposed to speak about "Meaningful Things"—but to speech that is motivated by craving, hostility, or other mental distortions. Idle gossip is pointless, but in a muted, gradual way it's also damaging. Tibetan teachers say that it's the least harmful of the ten nonvirtues, and the easiest way to waste a whole life.

8. Avoid malice, or ill will. This state of mind is so painful to experience, it's amazing that people ever indulge in it at all. It's like having a snake in your lap, or eating excrement. Why would we ever want to give it two seconds if we had noticed it in the first? It's terrible to wish another sentient being harm. Wishing them to suffer hurts us.

9. Avoid avarice. This is not just desire; if I'm thirsty I desire water, and that's fine. Avarice is craving for something that belongs to somebody else, not wanting them to have it because I want it.

10. Finally, avoid what are called false views. This refers not to doctrine, whether Buddhist, or Christian, or Hindu, or atheist, but to a mindset that denies fundamental truths. For example, a false view is the belief that our actions are inconsequential—that it doesn't really matter how we behave because things are controlled by chance or by fate, so we may as well just get by and have a good time. That is totally false, but people believe it, to varying extents. They think we can act or speak in certain ways with no repercussions. To shift to Buddhist terminology, it would be a denial of the truth of *karma*. *Karma* means action, and the law of *karma* is that actions have results. To deny this is just a view, but a view that can modify an entire life.

These ten precepts are simple, but they can be followed, and they set up a foundation in which the rest of these sometimes exalted practices and transformations of experience can take place. Without these simple things, we are probably just building sandcastles.

It's interesting to note that they are all negative restraints: "Avoid this." It doesn't say be good, or tell the truth. The negative approach indicates the quality of protection. We have something very precious—our life, our mind, our *buddha*-nature, our goals and aspirations—and we want to protect these. By simply avoiding the ten nonvirtuous actions, you create a space for this little plant to grow. With this kind of protection, a little practice, a little concern, it grows into a redwood tree which after a while doesn't need any protection at all. It provides protection to other creatures. In this way, ethical discipline is temporary insofar as it requires effort. As our own potential becomes manifest, as the wholesome qualities become stronger, then discipline falls away, because the virtue of our own mind is then protecting itself. An enlightened being can be utterly spontaneous at all times, without any restraint at all.

In the meantime, if ill will or other afflictions arise—sarcasm, cynicism, selfishness, pettiness—ideally we restrain them (contrary to some psychology that one hears). Sometimes the mind is dominated by such afflictions: they rush in and the mind takes on that flavor. Śāntideva, the very well known Indian *bodhisattva* of the eighth century, counsels us to pause and do nothing when we note that our minds are dominated by an affliction.[3] He did not say repress it, or pretend it's not there. Just pause, be present, and wait until it passes. It's like falling into delirium. That's not the time to go out and buy a house, or get married. Pick another time, but not while you're delirious. While you're delirious you just stay in bed and wait until you get well. The restraint of not acting at that moment is a gift to everybody.

Simple restraint lays a foundation. But in and of itself, it will not suffice. Restraint does not mean eradication. Merely pausing is not to eradicate the problem in itself. It's like placing yourself in quarantine when you fall ill. The illness spreads: if I feel nasty, and I speak with nastiness, it's like a contagious disease. There may be some people who have a strong spiritual immune system, and they just say, "Alan's being nasty, I hope he gets over it quite soon." Other people may not handle it so well, in which case it is infectious. I don't literally give it to them, but I provide a catalyst that sparks it. But to quarantine an individual or a group of people is not to heal them. It's a gift to everybody else, and it's a gift to those who are ill because they don't really want to spread it. Once you have applied the quarantine of ethics, something else is required for the cure.

THE AFFIRMATION OF INTUITIVE WISDOM

Note that our approach thus far is working with negation: Here is a problem; can we get rid of it? Can we get rid of delusion, instability, self-centeredness, injury, and so forth? Can we remove suffering from our experience? What you wind up with is a lack: a lack of suffering. The advantage of starting with such an approach, for people who are very critical and skeptical, is that you start with what you know. You probably have no doubt that you have experienced suffering and are still vulnerable to it. But that is not the only possible way to proceed. We do have intuition. You may sense that something has a good quality to it and holds a real promise, without being able to claim that you know it for a fact. In this case you start with an affirmation of intuition.

This focus on opening up to the intuitive wisdom that's already there is a different mode of Buddhist practice, and one which we find in other traditions as well. In this mode, presented in the Dzogchen and Mahāmudrā teachings, spiritual maturation is not so much a matter of inquiring and penetrating, or cultivating certain qualities. All the insight, all the love, all the realization we need is already latently present. They are already there on the level of our *buddha*-nature, in the essential nature of our own consciousness. They are just being obscured. You don't need to gain anything. Anything you gain is going to be lost at death anyway so it's not going to be very significant in the big picture. This is an affirmative path, not focusing on how to get rid of something, but how to

bring something to light. It's an affirmation that consciousness is one of the essential ingredients of this universe, of all
of existence, of all of reality. And the consciousness of every
sentient being bears limitless potential for compassion, insight,
and power. The whole of life and explicitly the whole of spiritual practice is simply designed to bring forth that potential.

The Buddha offered a metaphor for this in which he lik-
ened sentient beings like ourselves to atoms. Inside each atom
is a *buddha*. The Buddha who is manifestly present has only
one task: to take his *vajra* sledgehammer and split open these
atoms, so that what was latent now becomes manifest. The
Buddha is a cosmic atom-splitter and we are the atoms. This
entails a sense of discovery rather than cultivation, a simple
unveiling rather than an arduous effort at development. If the
heart leaps at hearing such an affirmation then that may be a
way you can follow. If your mind says, "Well, that's an interesting hypothesis, I wonder whether it's true," then you may
want to stay with the path of negation. If you don't question
the truth of suffering, the path of negation is a useful approach.
But if the heart leaps to affirm something beyond your knowledge, don't forsake it.

The question then becomes: How can we unveil this potential of the mind and uncover the wisdom, compassion, and
power of the spirit? What hinders the effulgence of this *buddha*-
nature? Things like injuring people, slander, abuse, lying, stealing, and killing stop it from springing forth. Stop these things,
and then the *buddha*-nature has a better chance to come out.
What else hinders it? Having a very scattered and dull mind,
a mind that oscillates between being excited and flopping over
in torpor; or a mind that's caught up in the ridiculous notion
that one's own well-being is a thoroughly individual matter,
to which everyone else's well-being is irrelevant. That's a big
obscuration, and it's clearly not true, so it would be good to
get rid of it. The notion that I exist as an autonomous ego, separate and isolated from others, like a little homunculus, also
obscures the mind. If you can get rid of all that and allow the

buddha-nature to arise spontaneously, this path culminates in the complete flowering of our lives and our minds, the complete manifesting of the jewel in the lotus that was there all along.

What would it mean to be a *buddha*, a spiritually awakened person? (A *buddha* is a type, not just a historical individual.) It is said that when the wisdom of the mind has been completely unveiled, you can raise a question, attend to it, and the truth will become evident. The mind is unimpeded. It's said that a *buddha's* compassion for every sentient being is like that of a mother for her only child, for whom she would gladly sacrifice her own life if necessary. It is a compassion without discrimination, that knows no bounds. Nice people don't get more of it than nasty people; animals get no less of it than human beings. It extends like an ocean: even, calm, embracing, and with an ocean's depth of concern and caring. And it's said that a *buddha's* mind has extraordinary power, a power that can engage with the physical world to transform reality.

Of these three aspects—wisdom, compassion, and power—the mind's power has perhaps been the most obscured in our civilization. Because we have followed such a materialistic bent, we have accomplished extraordinary feats in comparison to any other civilization. We have put rockets on the moon, built high dams, and burned holes in the ozone layer. We've done all kinds of incredible things. But in so emphasizing our material power, we have, perhaps inevitably, de-emphasized the power of the mind. We assume that a statement like, "...if you have faith as small as a mustard seed, you can say to this mountain, 'Move from here to there' and it will move. Nothing will be impossible for you,"[4] must be metaphor or totally goofy. But when Jesus said that, I suspect he was speaking literally of the power of the spirit.

There is the big picture. The foundation of ethical discipline is so simple in its essence that if we care for that foundation, then a lot will become evident without the need for a lot more information. But if we skip ethical discipline, the foundation is missing. Again, it's worth noting that it's a matter of restraint rather than doing good. When we try to avoid things that cause harm, the goodness arises in and of itself. We just have to give it a chance. Even though avoiding all those things may seem negative, the implicit message is very optimistic. Avoid harm and the wholesome quality inside will start to just burst forth.

In my experience, this is very ascertainable in relation to quiescence. Insofar as the mind becomes temporarily free of its turbulence and its torpor, and is able to find some stability with vividness, a sense of well-being and calm arises from the mind. This is something easily within reach, not some tremendous mystical realization. When you experience it for yourself, it gives you a sense of having inner resources and casts a very different light on all of your other desires. The whole laundry list of things you would like to do with your life—your occupation, where you want to live, the people you want to associate with, activities you want to engage in—are seen in a different light. It's not that they are devalued or abandoned, but if some of them collapse, you don't assume that your own well-being collapses as well. You know for yourself that well-being arises from the only source it has ever arisen from, the calm mind. A sense of freedom ensues from knowing that your well-being is not utterly dependent upon things that are entirely out of your control. That's a rather useful insight. External factors may catalyze a sense of well-being, or they may not. The only real hope is the quality of mind you bring to them.

A MEDITATION ON THE JEWEL IN THE LOTUS: OM MAṆI PADME HŪṂ

The jewel in the lotus is a wonderful metaphor for the essential nature of the mind. It integrates two very different approaches, recognizing that there is a worthy role for striving, for engaging in methods, for growth and development; and at the same time recognizing that all these methods are fundamentally designed simply to bring to light what is already there, in all of its perfection, in all of its completeness. This is the pure fountain of loving-kindness and wisdom we are trying to cultivate.

The *mantra* OM MAṆI PADME HŪM is associated with Avalokiteśvara, the embodiment of enlightened compassion, and the *mantra* is the verbal articulation of that same quality of compassion. Among the many interpretations of this *mantra*, here is one I find especially meaningful. Oṃ signifies the manifest body, speech, and mind. Maṇi in Sanskrit means "jewel." Padme, pronounced *pémé* in Tibetan, means "in the lotus." Hūṃ, pronounced by the Tibetans as *hoong*, is a syllable suggestive of the deepest, essential, transcendent nature of consciousness. So the *mantra* starts out from the manifest state of the body, speech, and mind, then through the metaphor of the jewel in the lotus, goes to the depths of consciousness.

As you chant the *mantra*, let your imagination come into play. The metaphor of the lotus is that of a flower that springs forth from the mud, from some dark and gooey ooze. It rises through the water and then finally emerges into the sunlight, bursting into blossom. Imagine, as the lotus opens up, right in the middle of it is a jewel. The lotus is the unfolding of our lives: the evolution of our own body, speech, and mind; our spiritual maturation from lifetime to lifetime; our development towards enlightenment. This metaphor for growth and movement towards spiritual awakening carries the nuance: "Strive diligently!" It carries a lot of emphasis on method and listening to teachings: "What are the proper methods? How do I counter these difficulties? How do I move past this obstacle?" This developmental approach is directional, a development towards something.

At the same time, as this lotus opens up, the jewel is right there in the middle. It has been there all along, even when the lotus was a closed bud submerged in the ooze. That jewel is the *buddha*-nature. The jewel is not developing: you don't need to add anything to it at all, and you can't subtract anything from it at all. It only needs to be discovered or revealed, so you can see what is already there.

As you chant, bring out the poetry in the practice and use the imagery of the metaphor. Imagine this jewel of the purity and perfection of your own *buddha*-nature. Imagine it as a pearl of white light emanating from your heart and suffusing your body. It's not just a physical light like turning on a light bulb, but a light that embodies and expresses purification, joy, and compassion. Imagine it coming from an inexhaustible source, saturating your body, suffusing and transmuting your body. Your body becomes the very nature of this light: not simply blood, organs, tissue, and bone with some light glowing through, but a body transformed into a body of light that emanates from your heart.

When your body is completely saturated, then let the light spread forth in all directions. Use this as an opportunity to bring to mind areas of the world that you think are really in need of some light. Send it out there, and imagine this light bringing the very same qualities of purification, joy, and compassion to those individuals or communities that most need it.

QUESTIONS AND RESPONSES:
ON ETHICS AND THE SEQUENCE OF PRACTICE

Question: When you mentioned ethics, you caught me completely blindsided. I want very much to block this out and pretend I don't have to adjust my daily life. That's where the rubber hits the road, so to speak. Either you change your lifestyle or you don't. My understanding of ethics means cutting back on the sensory stimuli in a culture which is sensorially incredibly assaultive and rich. It troubles me that among the meditation teachers I have encountered so far, it's almost as if they avoid pushing ethics very hard so as not to scare people away. But then I see my mind doing the same thing, so I wonder if we're shining a light on something that has to be spoken about.

Response: It's an issue I'm very familiar with. There are three major emphases in traditional Buddhist practice. The first unquestionably is ethics. The second is stabilizing the mind, and the third is insight practice. All too often, the first hardly even gets mentioned. We go straight for the cultivation of insight, and never mind the kid's stuff.

Question: Isn't that based on the false view that we are independent and therefore ethics don't really count?

Response: Yes. It's precisely that, a false view. It forgets that we are embodied in an environment and that we are interacting with other people. To avoid ethics because it doesn't sell well is pandering. Why is this happening? Is it just that the meditation teachers are trying to make a living, and they're afraid they'll get fired? A more charitable way to look at it is that we have been raised in a culture where the flavor of ethics is puritanical. Ethics means abstaining from a whole bunch of fun stuff that you're not supposed to do. We've all heard about the Ten Commandments, and then we hear that Buddhists are also supposed to abstain from ten nonvirtues.

But perhaps there is a sufficiently skillful way to introduce this so that people can start to experience some of the benefit of the practice. Consider a ten-day Vipassanā retreat, where the teacher doesn't harp on ethical principles, but just says: "Here's the technique, try it out." So many people come away from a ten-day retreat with their lives changed by real insights that open up avenues of experience they never knew were possible. They didn't get sledgehammered with ethics or with the discipline of stabilizing the mind, but they came away with something of value. That's precious. But when you take that home, it's fragile. You watch the half-life of your meditation practice as it decomposes after the retreat.

This raises an interesting question, and the answer might be useful in a way that a dogmatic dose of ethics is not. There was something of value and now it's deteriorating. What are the causes of the deterioration? It's hard to have much insight when the mind is turbulent. Some stability would be helpful. We'll come back to insight, but let's stabilize the mind first and make it more serviceable. So we do the quiescence practice for a while. If you do a good one-week *śamatha* retreat, you will very possibly find in that time better stability of mind, continuity of attention, and calm well-being than you've ever had in your life before.

But why does that calm deteriorate after the retreat? Perhaps you got really irritated one morning, shouting out the car window at someone who cut you off in traffic. When you came home, it was impossible to meditate. You sat there with your mind disgruntled and scattered. It would have been helpful not to have had that outburst. Maybe a slight shift in lifestyle would create a more fertile environment, so that when you achieve some degree of stability, your mind isn't immediately destabilized as soon as you return to your everyday life. Nothing creates such a chaotic turbulence in the mind as malice. This brings us back to the very bedrock of ethics as understood in Buddhism: try not to injure yourself, and try not to injure others. At the very least, avoid injury. This has nothing to do with turning off the television or abstaining from sensual pleasures. There's nothing necessarily injurious in that. To pig out on ice cream may not be all that healthy, but you're not doing anybody else damage. If you are, it's very subtle. It's nothing compared to becoming enraged, or insulting somebody viciously. It's said that a *bodhisattva* is willing to put up with a little bit of sensual indulgence if necessary, but there's no tolerance at all for hostility and aggression if they arise in his or her mind. If you want to indulge in a vacation, that's not a problem. Come back refreshed and then get back to your practice. But hostility and aggression are not a vacation; they destroy the practice.

Noninjury does entail some attention in day-to-day life, not just half an hour of meditation in the morning. It requires an ongoing introspection throughout the course of the day. It's so easy to let a word slip out that is a verbal punch. Devious or deceptive speech can slip out so quickly, let alone an injurious thought. Attend to those. When you see the impulse come up, just release it without expression.

Another aspect of this involves simplifying one's life. This entails a pervasive re-orienting of lifestyle, gradually withdrawing from sensual indulgence. The friendly way to do this, as opposed to the severe, puritanical method, is to experience another source of happiness. *Śamatha* can do that. The loving-kindness practice, also, can provide such a fullness of the heart that you reach the point where you would rather spend time practicing than watch a good movie on the television. The practice is actually more satisfying, so the choice becomes easy. That's a much better way to release sensual indulgence than through sheer determination, which can wind up as self-punishment. I've done that at times. On my first *śamatha* retreat, I found many wrong ways to practice, and that was one of them. I starved myself for pleasure, living in a hut that was saturated with bedbugs, fleas, and rats, with a totally uninteresting diet, and meeting with nobody. For a while I was deriving no pleasure at all from my practice. I was pile-driving with such intensity, determination, and discipline that there was no space for any happiness to squeak through.

There was not much benefit in this very strong asceticism. It would have been much more helpful to create some space. Even a novel or some candy bars would have helped. A gentle approach works better. It doesn't need to be severe or tyrannical. As we find more and more satisfaction, a sense of well-being, a sense of quiescence arising from the practice, then we can start to slough off the indulgences, because they are seen as futile. We don't need them anymore. But we do need to attend to the timing. Am I ready to release this now, or is it going to be experienced as deprivation? If it's experienced as deprivation, releasing it is probably premature. But if the indulgence seems redundant or pointless, it probably is. And that is the time to drop it.

Question: I've found that even the precepts that we express negatively and put into action negatively sometimes give a feeling that is completely positive. That can come as a surprise. I've approached something thinking: I'm going to deny myself this because it's for the best in the long run. But when I actually put it into action the feeling is incredibly positive. It's like you've just gone through a window, like a feeling of being free from an addiction.

Response: Precisely. It really is freedom. All of this is a path *of* freedom, and not just a path *to* freedom. One of the first things that happens is we begin to be able to free ourselves from compulsive behavior that only brings us injury.

Chapter Two
Entering *Śamatha* Practice

What impedes the flowering of loving-kindness, compassion, and other qualities that move us forward on the spiritual path? I have no simple answer, but something that definitely bears on the issue is the sense of inadequacy with which we engage with other people as we venture into life. We tend to engage with a sense of need: I need a job. I need love. I need affirmation. I need affection. I need respect. I need more money. I need more possessions. I need more happiness. This is the realm of the eight mundane concerns.[5] There's nothing wrong with needing something, in and of itself, but a sense of inadequacy and incompleteness is not conducive to a heart of loving-kindness. The mind that reaches out to other people, to the environment, to provide what it seems to lack itself, is a mind that is ignorant of its own resources for peace and happiness.

When *śamatha* practice is nested in a proper context, it's possible to recognize through something as simple as the breath that our own minds have an avenue to serenity and peace. And from that peace of mind, that sense of ease and contentment, being simply present with something as frankly uninteresting as the breath, there arises a happiness and satisfaction. The satisfaction comes from a very simple source: a mind that's not being pummeled to death with afflictions, craving, hostility, and aversion. We just don't normally give ourselves this break. Being endowed with consciousness in this universe, we are like a person sitting on a hill in a little shack, trying to eke out a bare living on the surface, not knowing that six inches underneath the dirt floor of our hut is a treasure, a vein of gold that just goes on and on. It's there already. We have no reason to feel needy. We have all the resources we need.

So discover that. Don't just believe it, but discover it experientially. We can bring forth a sense of serenity and well-being just in being present. Know that that's available. This is not to say that we don't want to have a spouse, or a job, or a car. But it casts them all in a different light. It's like taking the whole planet and shifting it so it's now rotating on a different axis. Everything doesn't fall off the planet, but there is a big shakedown when we recognize for ourselves that we bring enormous resources to every life situation. We bring something to offer, and not just neediness.

Samatha is immensely fertile ground for developing this. It's very useful for the cultivation of loving-kindness and compassion, and for learning to "touch the world lightly." I can't imagine the possibility of touching the world lightly without having recognized your own resources. An example is a true story from one of my teachers who recently passed away, the wonderful Lama, Tara Rinpoche. He was Abbot of the Tantric College in Assam in northeastern India, where some of the monks were quite formidable meditators. One in particular had left the monastery and was living in a little hut in the jungle where there were a lot of cobras. Tara Rinpoche was concerned for his student, so he gathered some sticks from a plant that was known to repel snakes and told him to plant them in the ground around the hut. The monk responded, "It's very gracious of you to give these to me, but I really don't need them. The cobras and I are getting along quite well. There's one living under my bed, and one behind the door." He knew of course that humans are not natural prey for cobras, and the only business they have with us is fear. But this man was not fearful, so he didn't arouse the aggression of the cobras. Nor did the cobras arouse aggression in him. They were just neighbors, and he felt there was no reason to repel them. He simply watched where he stepped. That indeed is touching the world lightly.

The whole point of *śamatha* is to make your mind serviceable. This means that however you wish to put your mind to service, it is now fit for the purpose. Whether it's for teaching, for meditation, for composing music—whatever you need to do—you now have a mind that is really functioning well. Until you have accomplished *śamatha*, the mind is said to be "dysfunctional." This dysfunctional mind is heavy, stiff, rigid, dark, and prone to grouchiness. Whatever virtue you wish to cultivate, the mind balks. The serviceable mind, in contrast, is buoyant, light, stable and clear, and ready to devote itself to the cultivation of wholesome qualities.

BEGINNING THE MEDITATION

Release the creations of the imagination and let the conceptual mind come to rest. Bring your awareness into the moment, without slipping off to fantasies about the future or recollections of the past. Let your awareness abide in the moment, in your body, quietly witnessing the tactile sensations throughout the body: the pressure of your legs, thighs, and buttocks against the ground; up through your torso, up through the head; the sense of warmth or coolness; any sensations of tingling or vibration. Let your awareness settle in this field of tactile sensations, resting there like a baby in a cradle.

Passively witness the sensations associated with the in-breath, throughout the entire course of the inhalation. Then follow the sensations associated with the out-breath throughout the entire course of the exhalation. The breath throughout this practice should not be controlled or manipulated, with one stipulation: relax the abdomen, especially the lower abdomen. Soften it so that you can feel the inhalation begin from the lower abdomen. If it's a shallow breath, you feel only the lower abdomen expand; a deeper breath expands from the lower abdomen upward, and the diaphragm expands; a still deeper breath moves from the abdomen to the diaphragm, and up into the chest. But let it begin from the abdomen, so that you are not breathing just in the chest.

Find the area at the nostrils where you notice the tactile sensations during the inhalation. Then, as the mind becomes attuned to this, note the tactile sensations following the in-breath, and just prior to the out-breath. Then note the sensations at the same spot during the out-breath. Place your mind there, like placing a baby in a cradle. At the beginning, you have a sense of rhythm, the oscillation of in-breath, out-breath, in-breath, out-breath. Let your awareness rest in this soothing place.

RELAXATION, STABILITY, AND VIVIDNESS

There are three points of emphasis in *śamatha* practice—relaxation, stability, and vividness—and it's very important to address them in sequence.

The first emphasis is on inducing a sense of relaxation of the body and mind: a relaxation of the awareness. This is not a forced, tense, or directed concentration, but rather one that allows the awareness to rest in the field of tactile sensations, in the rhythm of the in-breath and the out-breath. Because of its deep habituation and many impulses, it is difficult for the mind to remain at rest for very long. Your attention is bound to be drawn away, propelled into imagination, recollection, some discursive line of thought, desire, or emotion. If you find that your mind has been carried away, see if you can release the effort that is already being exerted in carrying the mind away. Especially on the out-breath, try releasing that effort, as if with a sigh of relief and release. Let go of those mental constructs, and let your awareness once again come to rest in the uncontrived, unconstructed tactile sensations of the moment.

For the first sessions, don't be concerned with stability, which implies continuity of attention. Don't be concerned with clarity, or vividness of attention. These will come in time, but to begin with, just see if you can respond to mental agitation and distraction not by clamping down but by releasing the effort that is sustaining the agitation. Come back and let the awareness rest in the gentle rhythm of the in-breath and out-breath, and feel the tactile sensations throughout the body.

Let your respiration be unforced and unmanipulated: let the body breathe itself. Especially during exhalation, take the opportunity to release the effort you may be giving to distracted thought or mental wandering. Let these mental constructs blow away like autumn leaves in a breeze, and continue to relax and release right into the end of the exhalation. Continue this right into the beginning of the inhalation. Don't suck the air in, but rather relax into the in-breath, witness it passively, as if the body is "being breathed."

A problem may arise in that, as soon as you focus on your breathing, it seems that you can't avoid manipulating it with effort or will. This raises a very interesting question: Can we attend to something closely without an almost irrepressible urge to control it? Does this have any relationship to our urge to control other areas of our lives? This is not just a little problem, but a challenge that really is mainstream practice. The way you can begin to crack the problem is to relax more into the exhalation. You don't have to blow out. You know perfectly well that exhalation will happen all by itself. When you breathe out, savor that. It feels so nice just to be effortless. Even a dying person can breathe out.

Then, from the out-breath, just melt right into the in-breath. See if you can maintain the same sense of relaxation and release right into the in-breath. Take that surge like a surfer, riding the out-breath right into the in-breath without any paddling. The most important point is the turnaround when you just start the in-breath. It can be interesting to note very distinctly the times when you miss and suck in the breath, and compare those to the times when it just flows in. Compare a failure and a success so you know the difference.

Posture is very important. If you are slumped over, compressing your diaphragm, then your abdomen can't expand very easily. It's crunched like an accordion and you have just a little bit of chest to breathe with. So without exaggerating, sit upright so that your abdomen can expand effortlessly and you can just go along with it.

The supine posture, lying flat on your back, can also be very helpful for this practice. There is a difference between this position and simply lying down as if you were about to take a nap. Most important is that your body should be in a straight line. You can check by bringing your heels together and raising your head to look down and visually align the point between your heels, your navel, sternum, and nose. Let your feet drop out to the sides. If space allows, you can extend your arms at about thirty degrees. Give a gentle extension to your spine by pulling your buttocks down slightly towards your feet. Similarly you can extend the spine by raising your head and drawing your chin down slightly towards your sternum. This should give a slight extension, nothing exaggerated. Experiment for yourself with your eyes. Some people prefer to close their eyes completely, others find it helps to leave the eyes partially open and let in a little bit of light to avoid getting spaced out. Relax the shoulders, relax the muscles of the face, and especially, just as in a sitting posture, let the eyes feel soft. Let your gaze grow still and your eyes rest, not protruding, not tight, but relaxed.

Make it a point to experience each breath as an adventure, an exploration to see whether you can completely relax in a full cycle. A full cycle would be a great accomplishment, from the out-breath all the way through the in-breath. And of course, by the time you've finished the in-breath, you're ready for the next out-breath. Now you're on the downhill slope of the roller coaster, and you can easily do the next stage. See if you can just maintain that continuity.

The next big shift in the practice is to move from relaxation to a sense of continuity, from breath to breath to breath. At this point, gross excitation (*auddhatya*) is the main problem. Gross excitation occurs when, while trying to follow the breath, the mind disengages from the breath and attends to something else entirely. Then after this little excursion you come back to the breath perhaps seconds or even minutes later. You may attend to the breath for another second, maybe even two seconds, then you're off someplace else. Gross excitation is simply lack of continuity. You've forgotten that you're meditating, and you're just sitting there thinking about something else. Subduing gross excitation entails staying on the object with greater continuity, for longer and longer periods: five, ten, fifteen seconds, and on.

But as you move towards stability, it's important to approach it gently. When I went on my first *śamatha* retreat, I pounded my way through like a pile driver, with no sense of maintaining a sense of ease. I began with a great deal of enthusiasm, but about ten times more determination than was called for, and I didn't even know that relaxation was particularly important. In the long run it was very exhausting. It would have been helpful if someone had said to me, "Oh, and by the way, hang loose."

It is important to sustain a sense of gentleness and ease, especially if you are impatient for results. The Tibetan Buddhist tradition strongly emphasizes the preciousness of a human life in which we have the opportunity and freedom to engage in spiritual practice leading to the elimination of suffering and its sources. It tells us that our present opportunity is incredibly rare and precious beyond all value, so we must take advantage now! This sense of urgency is all very well, as long as you keep a lightness and buoyancy to it. If we start combining the urgency with a grim-faced determination, it's likely to make us sick. Ultimately, the most important thing in practice is the continuity. It is not at all helpful to be marking the clock, thinking: "Can I accomplish *śamatha* in one year or two years, or before I die, or before I get old?"

Of course this is true not only of *śamatha*—of stabilizing awareness and making the mind into a serviceable tool—but of all Dharma practice. If we establish continuity in the main core of our practice—in the cultivation of compassion, of insight, of faith—if we practice these with continuity, we don't need to worry. Continuity means attending to them like a gardener who has planted a little stand of redwood trees, tending them from day to day, week to week, month to month, year to year. If we make swift progress in the practice, that's great. But even if we don't, it's not that important. If the continuity is established, then the life will run its span. The body will get worn out; the awareness will continue and will become embodied once again. That continuity is the most precious cargo we bring with us, because it will open up opportunities in the next life, and we can continue from there. If we are sporadic in the practice, taking a shotgun approach, blasting away over here and then forgetting about it, then blasting away at something else, who knows what kind of blast we will have in the next life?

In *śamatha* practice, once you have established stability within relaxation, then you can apply more concerted effort. This should be a fine-tuned effort, not a gross muscular effort. Aim to sustain somewhat greater continuity, but without the body/mind tightening up. When you're free of gross excitation, even temporarily, there is a calm and stability in your awareness, acting like the ballast of a ship. When you have relatively good continuity, in which you simply don't lose the object perhaps for five, ten, fifteen, twenty minutes, or maybe even longer at a stretch, then it's almost certain that some laxity (*laya*) will set in. It may feel like a complacency, a settling in. It's called sinking, like sinking back into an easy chair, saying "Well, I guess this is what I'm supposed to do." At that point we need to recognize that the task isn't finished yet. There is a third ingredient without which we will never get to *śamatha* or open up the full capacity of the mind. Vividness is the final, crucial component.

People develop in *śamatha* practice at varying rates, and also in various ways. It's possible to make generalizations, but they may not apply to all individuals. Having said that, as a generalization, there is a strong temptation to seek out vividness too soon. It gives you a *high* in the old-fashioned '60's sense of the term. There is a pleasure in it and everything becomes extraordinarily interesting. But if the vividness lacks an underlying stability, it is fragile and tends to collapse very easily. And so, because the vividness is so enticing, it is generally sound advice to develop stability first. Likewise, it is usually helpful to emphasize relaxation before stability, because there is a common tendency, especially among Western meditators, to bring a lot of effort to the practice initially. Discipline is valuable, but not if you sacrifice a sense of ease in the practice.

Generalizations aside, not everybody is a beginner, and even those who may be starting fresh in the practice sometimes develop quite quickly. If, in the course of a session, your sense of ease is sustained, you maintain focus on the object with stability, and the continuity is really quite good, you may find yourself beginning to sink into the object. This is a premature phasing out of duality, merging with the object in a way that is not useful, like slipping down into mud. At that point, it's time to exert more effort and increase the vividness. The practice then becomes a dance, enhancing the vividness but not at the cost of the stability; just as it was a dance to bring in greater stability but not at the cost of relaxation. When the continuity is lacking, and you still have to deal with a lot of turbulence, that's not the time to worry much about vividness. If you try to attend to vividness at this stage, it will probably just make the mind even more turbulent, with little flashes of vividness but no foundation.

When continuity is established, sinking into laxity is the main challenge. And if laxity goes farther, it progresses to lethargy (*styāna*), in which you just feel heavy. Beyond lethargy is sleepiness (*middha*), when you begin to nod off. With laxity you have just lost the edge, you're not falling asleep yet. When you find the first trace of laxity setting in, it's time then to attend more closely, to take a greater interest in the object of your meditation. It may also be a time to bring in some outside help, such as imagining flooding your body with light. Or if you find yourself even a little on the warm side, take off a layer of clothing, or drink a glass of cool water, or wash your face with cold water. Of course, make sure that you have enough sleep. If you're not getting enough sleep at night, it's a no-win situation. Meditation is not a substitute for sleep. You may find that if your meditation is going well you don't need as much sleep, but don't cut off sleep to see if you can meditate a little bit longer. That won't work in the long run.

If laxity or lethargy become chronic, then go back to discursive meditation for a while, and attend to subjects that inspire you, that uplift and invigorate the mind. If you find that none of those techniques work, then you may want to switch objects altogether. Breath awareness is good for a lot of people, but not for everyone. For those who visualize fairly easily, there's another whole route to *samatha* through visualization. That's much more common in the Tibetan tradition than breath awareness.[6] If you are practicing visualization, then the treatment of laxity is straightforward: just put another hundred volts into your visualized object. Brighten up the illumination.

QUESTIONS AND RESPONSES: ON BREATH AWARENESS

Question: I've learned to meditate on the breath with an awareness of the breath moving through the whole torso, rather than just the tactile sensations at the nostrils. Can I practice *samatha* with this type of whole-body awareness?

Response: Following the breath in and out through the whole torso, through the rise and fall of the abdomen, is one of various avenues to breath awareness. It's good for stabilizing at the gross level but it probably will not take you all the way to *samatha*. It's not ideal for a deeper level of stabilization because there is too much motion, too much vacillation. If it's helpful at the beginning, that's fine, but you don't want to stop there. Focusing on the breath at the nostrils does work, I have confidence in that. Shifting techniques is a question of habituation. I'm not saying, "Now don't pay any attention to that whatsoever. See only this." But make your choice and the rest will take care of itself.

Question: What should we do if we find that at the end of exhalation there tends to be a lag time before inhalation begins, maybe ten or fifteen seconds, maybe more?

Response: As a matter of fact, there is a *prāṇāyāma* technique in which you consciously rest for ten to twenty seconds at the end of each exhalation and also each inhalation. You would do that for a maximum of fifteen minutes as a *prāṇāyāma* technique. Here it's not planned, but it often happens that excess tension in the body and mind percolates out in this way. This is not a problem at all, as long as it occurs only occasionally. But if this happens regularly, and you find at the end of the session that your body-mind feels heavy or sluggish, then it's a fairly clear indication you are doing it too much. You have to judge for yourself. If you find that you just feel very present and grounded, that's fine. But if it causes a lethargic feeling, then ease off.

Your posture can make a difference here. Sitting relatively straight but with a slightly bowed spine compacts the diaphragm ever so slightly. In this casual posture it comes naturally to pause at the end of the out-breath. Then finally, like climbing up hill, the breath comes back into the torso and revitalizes the system. Raising the posture slightly to lift the diaphragm can prevent this happening to excess. The breath will flow in more easily and you will find that it invigorates you. When your breath gets into a rhythm and moves like a flower blossoming up into your torso, it's very soothing and invigorating at the same time, even therapeutic for the body and mind.

Question: How do you stop yourself from willfully affecting the breath when you are so aware of it?

Response: If you surrender yourself to the practice, it's not as much of a problem as you might imagine. Otherwise it would be horrendously difficult, because the breath becomes very subtle, which means it also becomes as easy to manipulate as a feather. Although the breath awareness in itself is not strictly a *vipaśyanā* practice, insight does enter into this. If we can attend so closely to something that is so delicate and yet not manipulate it with our will, but just rest with it; if the attention and breath can move like two dancers, without one grabbing the other and pulling it around, there is not much space left for a gross sense of ego. The fine-tuning of this requires you to be so much in the moment that you are very near insight practice. My teacher Geshe Ngawang Dargyey once told me that if you actually accomplish *śamatha*, it's relatively easy to develop radically life-transforming insight.

Question: After just a little while of counting my breath, I fade out and I don't come to until you ring the bell. Is this what you mean by laxity?

Response: It is. If you are simply fatigued, it's better to rest. When you find that regardless of how much you apply yourself, the mind is just not up to the task, the problem may be fatigue. It may also have a lot to do with the degree of interest in the practice. If you are really not very interested, it may be an inappropriate practice. It's worth discussing that with a teacher. A traditional response would be to keep the sessions fairly short. Then, if your interest wanes, you don't simply hang out and waste time. You can waste time very easily in individual practice when you're on your own. Variety is another thing that can be helpful. If you are bored, try breaking up the practice with discursive meditation, alternating the *śamatha* with a more active mode of practice.

But in defense of *śamatha*, if by any means, whether short sessions or recalling your motivation, you can start to get the taste of vividness along with continuity of attention, the meditation starts to reap its own rewards. The practice itself gives you its own well-being, and you no longer need to look for outside help to motivate you. When the practice is rewarding in itself, you have reached a watershed.

It is also helpful to bring a lot of light into the practice. Meditate in a brighter environment, a place where the light is softly bright. Inside as well, generate light in the practice. With your imagination suffuse your body with light and then let it spread out from the body. When the mind closes down, it needs to be countered with effort. Rather than relaxing into the problem, bring in some high-voltage awareness.

Question: During the last few sessions I had no awareness of my body at all. I was looking down at it like it wasn't mine. Is that detachment okay, or do you want to feel more connected to the body if, for example, you want to use the body of light technique?

Response: Those are two different questions. The disengagement from the body is just fine. The practice of bringing light into your body of light is a preamble. When the mind starts to enter more deeply into the meditative object, the sense of having a body at all will fall away, in which case you don't need to use the body of light. It has served its purpose, which was to get you to that point. That's one reason why good posture is so important: as you start to disengage from the body, it goes on auto-pilot. If you start it off in the right direction, it will maintain its own posture, taking care of itself into very deep *samādhi*.

Question: My back and my knees are painful from sitting. How should I deal with physical pain during the meditation?

Response: There are different views on how to deal with the pain that arises from sitting. One view, which I respect very highly, teaches that the pain is part of the practice. You will find this a lot in Zen and to varying extents in the Vipassanā tradition. You accept the pain without responding to it. You just let the waves of pain come through, while you maintain the practice. The Tibetan tradition, on the other hand, places little or no value on physical pain in the meditation. They say: If it hurts, move. We've got enough problems in our lives without inviting physical pain in the meditation. Of course, you can go overboard with this approach if you start to fidget at the slightest discomfort and scratch every little itch that comes up. Your awareness just decomposes. I would suggest a middle way, but the middle way that I teach and practice tends to be quite gentle. If you find something is really poking into your consciousness and nagging at you, then I suggest you move. You might try just a very subtle shift at first, perhaps just rearranging your weight. You may find that refolding your legs helps. If your body is just fatigued, your muscles are stressed, and it doesn't matter much which way you place your legs, the best thing is to move into the supine position. But don't move at the earliest sign of discomfort, because it would be good to be able to increase the bubble of comfort a little bit each time. Stretching that duration will give you more leeway for your practice.

I've been reading the very early literature about *śamatha* practice and its relationship to the path as a whole. It is very interesting that, as far back as the Buddha himself, you don't find themes like: "Strive diligently, I know it hurts a lot, but grit your teeth and try anyway." Instead the Buddha says, "And through the *śamatha* practice, joy arises, and from the joy, then insight arises..." I found that interesting. We do what we can to create the circumstances for a sense of happiness and well-being to arise in the mind. That's a wave you can ride on. All things being equal, I'd rather be riding a wave of happiness than a wave of physical misery.

Question: How does *śamatha* practice differ from breath awareness as taught in Vipassanā or the Theravāda tradition?

Response: First of all, you should note that the contemporary Theravāda tradition uses some terminology very differently from the way it is used in the Tibetan tradition and even in *The Path of Purification* by Buddhaghosa, which is the basis for the present teaching. You may sometimes hear the term *śamatha* used to describe a much more elementary state than what we are talking about here.[7]

Vipassanā, as it's currently taught in Southeast Asia and Sri Lanka, tends to emphasize simple mindfulness: being thoroughly in the present and letting your awareness be as free as possible from any conceptual overlay, including judgments, classifications, and especially, emotional responses. You simplify your awareness as much as possible, honing your mindfulness to a fine key. Whatever comes up—be it the birds singing, a thought, an emotion, tactile sensations, pain, pleasure—you watch it without judgment, without grasping on to it, without conceptually elaborating on it. This gives you a much clearer awareness of what is taking place in the moment. It does yield a type of insight, and it's enormously useful. It's also essentially very, very simple.

As one progresses in the practice, you may be encouraged to examine whether there is any "I" present in the phenomena you are observing, whether you find anything static or stable, or whether everything is in a state of flux. This is not analysis or philosophizing, but it is a mode of inquiry. *Vipassanā* is an insight practice, and traditionally it really does entail an inquiry into the nature of reality.

In contrast, *śamatha* does not involve inquiry, even though some of the methodology such as breath awareness may be similar. *Śamatha* is honing the tool of the attention. You're developing stability and vividness. If your stability or your vividness starts to wane, you apply an antidote. In *vipassanā*, if you find laxity arising, you simply note it. You don't try to counteract it or do anything about it at all. If you find your mind is getting turbulent, you note: "Aha, there are a lot of thoughts." You're succeeding right there, and you are not continually working on an agenda as in *śamatha*. That is a distinction in the qualitative experience of the two types of meditation.

There are people who believe, and I think in some ways with good grounds, that if you progress in the practice of *vipassanā*, the mind will become stable and your vividness will be enhanced as a result of the mindfulness and insight practices. *Vipassanā* can be a superb foundation for *śamatha*, just as *śamatha* can give you the stability and vividness you need to really benefit from insight practice. For some people, it may be more effective to do mindfulness continuously and do very little sitting meditation. If you can develop the kind of mindfulness that blankets the whole day, then you will really have some capital to invest if you choose to do a *śamatha* retreat. And then, if you should go into another *vipassanā* retreat with the tools of *śamatha* already at hand, that's a combination that will be very effective. Obviously, *vipassanā* and *śamatha* are compatible.

THE MASTERY OF ATTENTION: MINDFULNESS AND INTROSPECTION

Much of the time our attention is compulsive. We don't really want to attend to distracting thoughts while we are meditating, and yet we do. The directing of awareness has a lot to do with will, but is not always will-driven. When it is compulsive it is probably object-driven. For example, if we become enraged, we may not want to be focusing on the thing that enrages us and yet that's exactly where the attention goes. It's not because of some external stimulus. We could be sitting alone in a room and yet the mind is compelled to attend to this enraging object. *Śamatha* is designed to give us not just control of attention, but freedom of attention. If we wish to attend to the breath, we have the freedom to attend to the breath. If we wish to attend to something else, we have the freedom to attend to that.

Mastery of the attention is an extraordinary feat. I have found William James' writings on attention to be very insightful.[8] But the Buddhists have a lot to say about it as well. In the Buddhist context the mastery of attention is more than a psychological accomplishment. Not only have you gained mastery in a very significant way over you own mind; mastering your attention starts to influence your environment as well. Śāntideva, for instance, declares that all manner of external dangers can be subdued by mastering one's own mind.[9]

When we find that the mind has become distracted, a traditional, time-tested solution is to simply take a greater interest in the main object. Attend to each breath as something utterly unprecedented: this breath will never come back. There will be another breath, but this one is unique. Attend to it with a playful quality and a light touch: "That was neat—two breaths in a row! How about three?" See if you can maintain this quality of attention without becoming heavy and morose, mouth grimacing under the discipline. Counting can be fun occasionally. See if you can get all the way to ten without ever falling off the breath. Then, if you've succeeded, go without counting for a while. Play with it, but don't make it conceptually elaborate. Insofar as you can take more interest in each breath, it's preferable to have interest that is uncomplicated rather than interest that is complicated.

There are two distinct qualities of awareness to cultivate in the *śamatha* practice: mindfulness (*smṛti*) and introspection (*samprajanya*). They are defined very specifically in the Tibetan Buddhist context, which is somewhat different from the Theravāda context. Mindfulness is that faculty or mode of awareness that is directly concerned with a familiar object, in this case the tactile sensations associated with the breath. In this practice, mindfulness is a continuum, an unbroken stream, attending to the in-breath, the out-breath, and also those interim moments between the breaths. The sole task of mindfulness is to attend to the object with continuity. It's like the beating of the heart: you always want it to be happening. If it's not there, then try to get it back as quickly as you can.

Introspection has a quite separate task from mindfulness. It serves rather like quality control in a factory. While mindfulness is attending to the meditative object, introspection is attending to the meditating mind, checking on how it's going: "Am I still trying to control the breath? Am I chattering about the breath as I'm watching it? Am I falling asleep? Am I spaced out?" Introspection also has the task of checking up now and again on the body. Check out the posture: the shoulders should be as relaxed as a coat on a hanger. Check that your face has not become tight, with the muscles around your eyes or jaws contracted. If you are accustomed to proper meditation, you may find that you have a reliable posture, and it doesn't need much introspection. In earlier phases of meditation, or if you are experimenting with different postures, attention to the body is more important. But the chief task of introspection is to monitor the mind, because the mind tends to change faster than the posture does.

Note that introspection is not on call all the time. You don't need to have quality control checking every single item that comes off the assembly line, but you do want it poking in intermittently. If the mind has become distracted, then it is the task of introspection to recognize this, and then you must apply your will to restore mindfulness. If you find that you're going into a slump in the meditation, that vividness is gone and you're drifting off, then it's the task of introspection to note that and arouse the will to deal with it. Maybe you're just tired and it's time to end the meditation, go for a walk, or do something entirely different; or maybe you need to pep it up a little bit and bring back the vividness.

Introspection needs to be more frequent in the earlier phases of the practice, both towards the mind and the body. Eventually you will learn to rest in a stable posture, and introspection will no longer be necessary for the body.

As you progress, introspection is not needed so often, but it must become more educated and more acute. The types of problems to attend to become more subtle. If you do the practice with some continuity, there's a possibility of actually getting better at it! After several months you may very well find that gross excitation is not much of a problem any more. Gross excitation or gross agitation occurs when mental distraction causes you to forget about your meditation object altogether. The breath is history and now you're thinking about ice cream, or pizza, or where you need to go at five o'clock.

When you get to a point in your meditation where gross excitation doesn't arise any more, you may still experience subtle excitation. Subtle excitation is the background chatter that appears around the edges of your attention even as you are focused on the object. It may entail mental chit-chat or imagery. Introspection remains intermittent, but it has to be enhanced.

You may continue even further to a point at which both gross and subtle excitation are gone and you can sustain mindfulness with finer and finer tuning. Think of the moments of awareness as a line of dominoes: the space between them gets

narrower and narrower. When the space, which is the space
between moments of mindfulness, is quite big, there is room
for subtle excitation in between the mindfulness, so you have
the sense of doing two things simultaneously. But as you start
to close the distance between the dominoes, there is no space
for other imagery. The line of dominoes becomes a seemingly
smooth, seamless surface of mindfulness on your object. As
you develop greater stability, and excitation decreases on both
gross and subtle levels, then laxity is almost bound to arise.
This feels like complacency. You are resting on the object and
the edge of awareness has gone. You may have some sem-
blance of vividness, but it's not that great. You are slacking
off. The Tibetan word for laxity (*bying ba*) literally means "sinking." You need introspection to detect this, and the remedy is
to give the meditation more intensity. I can only speak in metaphors now, but to counter gross laxity you need to close the
ranks a bit more and bring in a greater spark of vividness.
There is even a subtle degree of laxity in which the object remains vivid but without full intensity. (The only way to know
what I'm talking about is to go ahead and do the practice.
Otherwise it's like trying to describe chocolate to somebody
who has never tasted it.)

By the time that you've moved through gross and subtle
excitation and countered both gross and subtle laxity, you're
on easy street. From that point, you no longer need introspection. In fact, introspection then becomes a nuisance and de-
tracts from the meditation. It's not a line that you cross, but a
stage you move into gradually. There may be times even relatively soon in your meditation when you can honestly say, "I
don't need to do anything here. I don't need introspection. I
can just go with the flow." But don't be premature about this.

Note that introspection is auto-referential, a kind of inner
monitoring. When introspection is no longer needed because
the problems for which it was designed are no longer present,
at that point the reified sense of subject-object dichotomy begins to break down. You are left with just the experience, the
event of mindfulness taking place with continuity and with

vividness. It's from that space that you move right into the actual accomplishment of *śamatha*. That is an advanced state, but you will almost certainly experience facsimiles of that state prior to achieving it. You get glimpses, or brief tastes, when you know for yourself that, for a while at least, there is no longer a sense of the meditator. The dichotomy between the meditator and meditative object is something that has to be constructed: it's not a given. We construct it by conceptualizing it concretely, patting it into shape: "That's the object, this is the subject, this is the meditation, and I'm doing well—or not." Insofar as you release this ongoing commentary, you also begin to release the more quiet construct of "I am meditating." And you release it by simply attending more closely and with tighter continuity, moving the dominoes closer together, until there is no more space to also say, "And, oh yes, I am meditating."

ŚAMATHA AS A CATALYST FOR MENTAL EVENTS

Eventually you are bound to experience creativity surfacing in *śamatha*. Especially during a relatively stable meditation session, instead of being distracted by a current of rambling thoughts, just a few thoughts will come in that seem to be of real value. They may be innovations concerning something you've been working on, things you don't want to sweep out with the rest of the rubbish.

The very fact that it happens is interesting. When I was studying physics as an undergraduate at Amherst College (after being out of academia for fourteen years), I had been grinding my teeth for three hours on a problem in elementary mechanics, something about a cannonball breaking into three parts in midair, and trying to figure out where each part lands. I was a monk at the time, and the trajectory of cannonball fragments was low on my list of interests. Like a tractor pushing against a granite wall, spewing forth exhaust and fumes, I was getting nowhere at all except to a state of frustration. So I just stopped and went off to meditate. Fifteen minutes later, something surfaced: not a complete solution, but an opening,

like getting a knife into a clamshell. Whether *śamatha* meditation helps us solve a gritty problem, or opens up something
very wonderful in a creative field such as music or art, what
do we do with it?

You probably won't have a dozen valuable insights per
session, so you can probably remember them without jotting
them down. In my experience, it's enough to just hold the
spark of it. When you come out of the meditation you can let
that spark re-ignite. Of course, if it is just too hot to handle,
and you are too excited to meditate, then go with it. You may
get a full symphony orchestra with all the individual parts
clearly audible. Mozart described the experience of composing as writing down what he heard, like a scribe or reporter.
Do whatever you like with it and then come back with a sense
of completion.

Although breath awareness is not image-oriented, as the
mind becomes calm, the practice may catalyze images and
memories that are more vivid than any you have ever experienced. It may go beyond the visual to include aural and other
sensory impressions. The imagery may even have continuity
as well, as events unfold in your mind. You can sustain this
material that the meditation catalyzes if you want to. You may
even surprise yourself as to how long you can remain in it.
You might play with it, exercise it a little bit. But let images
come up spontaneously; don't pursue them. And if you are
really concerned with *śamatha*, then acknowledge them, and
release them on their way.

Some of the material that surfaces is likely to be traumatic
and bring a lot of agitation: memories that stir guilt, fear, rage,
or some deep resentment. As these memories, images, or emotions come up, they become your challenge. This is a major
event in the practice. It should be regarded not as a nuisance
or as a problem, but as a crucial and prominent facet of the
practice. That means you learn to acknowledge it, confront it,
bring understanding to it, accept it, and release it. It doesn't
mean that you hold on to it or let it overwhelm you. We don't
need to process every bad experience we've had in our life—

we would never finish. Simply releasing is optimal, but at times the experience may be more tenacious than that. If, for example, resentment keeps pounding on the door of your mind, maybe you need to do some loving-kindness practice to clear it out. Or if there is guilt, maybe you need to bring some understanding to unravel it. But if you can deal with it by simply releasing it, great!

DEALING WITH PROBLEMS IN *SAMATHA* PRACTICE

If your practice is wholesome and enjoyable, maintained with a sense of buoyancy and well-being, the chances are extremely remote that any problems that are catalyzed will become entrenched. I never heard of such a case. Almost every case I have encountered of persistent problems in *samatha* practice is characterized by a lack of buoyancy and a reliance on sheer discipline. Typically, when *samatha* practice goes wrong, it gets heavy—frustrating and isolated, barren and dark. You may feel you have to muscle your way through, and of course that makes it worse.

Physical tension, aches and pains, are not necessarily indications of a problem. In the early stages especially, tension in the body may be brought on more by the mind than by muscle fatigue, or some other purely physical factor. People's knees may hurt when they are meditating and feel fine at any other time, even if they are sitting motionlessly for long periods of time. Part of the mind wants an excuse. If the pain is caused by this sort of influence from the mind, then make a choice. Recognize that the tension is not really debilitating, and just let it go.

If the problem tends to linger between sessions, and especially if it's conjoined with an array of other symptoms that suggest an imbalance in your nervous system, you should be more careful. Such symptoms include tension, a feeling of darkness or heaviness at the heart that lingers, a gloom in the mind that may slip into depression or irritability, nervousness, and a tendency to weep—not a refreshing, cleansing weeping, but just grief. If you recognize one or more of those occurring in a chronic fashion, then something has gone wrong. It's time to lighten up, speak with the teacher, and clear it out. If you are on your own, the first thing to do is lighten up the intensity of the practice. Ease off and let yourself be a little bit lazy. You might try some yoga: that what it's for. Above all, bring in a greater sense of buoyancy and find something to restore good cheer and lightness to the mind. If you can do that, in all likelihood, you will knock out the problem. When the mind's joy, its buoyancy and lightness, becomes a distant memory, that's when these symptoms can really set in persistently and become problematic.

If you ever experience a dense, dark, tight, fisty quality, especially in the area of your heart or the center of your chest, back off immediately. Back off just as if you found a snake in your lap. It's really important not to pursue the meditation if this happens, as great damage can be done. Do something cheerful instead. Go eat pizza and ice cream; listen to your favorite music. Do whatever you can to bring lightness back in and get out of that space quickly.

Why would this happen? The heart center is closely connected to mental consciousness. There is a vital energy in the body that you can experience in a tactile way, even though it is not physical in the Western scientific sense. (There is no place for "vital energy" in modern physics. I don't think there ever will be; it's a different type of phenomenon. This is a type of "qualia" that is experienced first-hand, not something existing purely objectively, independently of experience.) But it manifests, among other ways, as the physical sensations at your heart that accompany different emotional states. When you feel buoyant and happy, when you feel excited, when you feel heavy and depressed, when you feel like dirt: check the physical sensations at your heart. For any of the major mind states, you can probably feel the corresponding vital energy if you attend to it.

In *śamatha* practice, you are doing something very unusual with and to your mind. You're asking it to focus on one thing and stay there. That means you are, in a sense, compacting your attention. You're channeling and collecting it, gathering it together. As you gather your mind, you also gather your vital energies, drawing them to the heart. If the quality of awareness that you are compacting has negative elements such as resentment, guilt, depression, sadness, or fear, that will also show up in the heart as a sensation of heavy darkness, a feeling like you have just swallowed a rock.

The Tibetans describe this as "bad energy" (*rlung ngan pa*), and of course that is just what it feels like. It is dangerous, because the energy can get lodged in the heart and stay there. That may lead to chronic depression, or worse. It's unfortunate, and it happens unnecessarily to too many meditators. You can work through it but it's difficult, and it's far better not to fall into it in the first place. If it does start, the sooner you deal with it, the easier it will be. How do you address it? You need to bring a lot of buoyancy and light into your life and you probably shouldn't meditate much. If you do meditate, the sessions should be very short and very light; loving-kindness practice is appropriate, but never to the point where it gets oppressive or heavy in any sense. You need to keep a lightness in your life, do things that you enjoy, spend time with people you enjoy. If you have a spiritual teacher, think about him or her a lot. Do whatever you can to introduce a quality of lightness, sweetness, and warmth into your heart and mind. You really have to take major steps to counter the dark, cold, heaviness of this problem, and be very patient about returning to any kind of intensive meditation. You have to take a leave of absence for a while.

It is unusual, but similar problems to those associated with the heart center can sometimes happen when breath awareness with a focus on the nostrils concentrates too much energy in the head. You may find your head feeling full and bloated like a pumpkin on top of your neck. Or you may experience a feeling of pressure in the head, or headaches. If this happens, drop that technique for a while. Bring the awareness down to the abdomen or diffuse it gently throughout the whole body, but get it out of the head. It's not healthy; if you continued slogging on with that technique, it could become a chronic problem and there is really no reason to let that happen. Headaches should not become common as a result of practice. If they occur once in a while, that's normal. But if you find you're getting headaches from meditation with any degree of regularity at all, then something is wrong and needs to be checked. If headaches become at all consistent, please speak with a qualified teacher.

On the other hand, you may experience many unusual physical sensations in *śamatha* practice that are not at all cause for concern. People commonly report bizarre experiences such as distortions of the sense of physical space, illusions of movement or falling, a sense that the limbs are contorted, or a ringing in the ears. You may feel as if your body is swelling up like the Pillsbury doughboy, or it may feel rooted to the earth. In general, when such experiences involve the whole body, or are peripheral, focused on the limbs, they are not danger signs at all, but quite harmless. The traditional instructions are to ignore such phenomena, hard as that may be. By paying attention to a sensation or becoming fixated on it, you perpetuate it and it can then turn into an obstacle.

The reason behind such experiences is that *śamatha* has a profound effect on the vital energy system in the body. We are doing something the mind is not at all accustomed to, plunking the mind down and saying: Stay! As you concentrate and channel the mind in an unfamiliar way, especially if you go to greater depths than you have previously, this is bound to have an effect on the vital energies. They start to rearrange themselves. This continues all through the course of developing *śamatha*, all the way to its culmination. When you actually attain *śamatha*, there is a radical shift of vital energies. It's like having your whole house rewired: the energies will function differently, and your body will feel extraordinarily light and pliant. From then on, unless you let your *śamatha* deteriorate, that becomes your normal physical state. Prior to the actual achievement of *śamatha* there's a lot of rearranging of the furniture, so to speak, as the energies shift around. And as this takes place, you may feel strange physical sensations, perhaps even as if your body is rotating or turning upside down.

What if you are not sure if something you are experiencing might be problematic? There are two types of teachers: one is your own intuition, the other is an outside source. If you have a very strong sense something is worth exploring, do so. Release yourself into it and experiment. If you have problems, come back and check with an outside source. If you have a recurring problem with headaches or a heaviness of the heart, I suggest you consult a qualified meditation teacher. If you ever start developing a chronic sense of fatigue and tension in the meditation, or a chronic sense of darkness around the mind, that's a time to stop and take appropriate countermeasures. Come and talk to a teacher. Get it early and nip it in the bud. Don't let it linger and become an embedded problem.

Not many people are able to do *śamatha* practice exclusively for an extended retreat. At times the mind inevitably gets heavy and needs to be inspired and uplifted. Alternating *śamatha* with loving-kindness meditation can help. Sitting back and reflecting on why you are doing this can be very helpful. Find ways of uplifting the mind without drawing it into hindrances. You might find it uplifting to think of a person you find extremely attractive, but then you are bringing desire into the meditation, and that comes with its own bundle of problems. Keep the relief wholesome. You might just take a walk, or talk to some friends once in a while. If they are doing the same practice as you are, it can be really inspiring.

The simple technique of bringing light into the meditation can be extremely helpful. Develop a sense of your own body as a body of light: a very calm, soothing, transparent light. It should be light in every sense of the term, buoyant as well as softly glowing, not at all dense, as if there were extra space between the molecules. Keep that sense of light as your environment, and within that attend to the sensations of the breath at the nostrils. See if you can relax into it. If you find some tension coming in, then temporarily withdraw a little from the intensity of your focus on the breath; set out into this diffuse lightness again, suffused with a sense of ease. Imagine if you really had a body of light, how comfortable that would be. Remain there for a while, and then keeping with that sense of ease and lightness, come back in to the focus on the breath.

Another very practical suggestion that Tibetan lamas offer, especially for this type of focused, concentrated practice in which the mind is drawn very much inward, is to spend the time between sessions in a place where you can gaze out for a long distance to a very far horizon.

Chapter Three
The Path to *Śamatha:* An Overview

THE NINE STAGES OF THE PATH TO *ŚAMATHA*

The Tibetan Buddhist tradition presents a very clear map of the path to *śamatha*, going all the way from the beginning of the practice to its culmination. It begins right here where your feet are now—not at the level of a super-monk or an advanced yogi—and it marks out a progression of nine distinct stages prior to the accomplishment of *śamatha*. Knowing the progression is helpful, but not because you should be marking your progress, competing against a standard, even against your own personal best. It is helpful because the problems that arise in each stage are distinct and require different remedies.

1. *Mental Placement*

Accomplishing the first stage means that you can find your object. You find it, the teachings say, by hearing about it: you hear what you are supposed to do, and then you do it. If you are studying under a traditional Tibetan teacher, you might well be instructed to take a statue of the Buddha, gaze at it, and then visualize it. If you can see the image in your mind's eye, you have accomplished the first stage. Doing breath awareness, you are told to attend to the tactile sensations of the passage of the breath at the apertures of the nostrils or above the upper lip. Some people don't get it immediately; they find nothing there. When you can direct your attention there, and feel some sensation—note when the breath is coming in, when the breath is going out—then you have accomplished it.

2. *Continual Placement*

Continual placement means that you are able to attend to your meditative object, free of gross excitation, for about a minute without forgetting it altogether. The Tibetans measure it as the time it takes to recite OM MAŅI PADME HŪM once around the rosary, or one hundred and eight times.

There's nothing magical about that duration, but maintaining such a degree of continuity is a signpost. It implies you have some actual continuity in your attention. At the first stage you have virtually no continuity at all. You pop in and out for a second or two at a time, a staccato meditation, and then you're gone for five or ten seconds. The second stage moves towards continuity, although there still can be plenty of peripheral noise. There's probably background chatter in the mind, and your object may not be very clear. It could be extremely fuzzy, but at least you're not losing it.

You accomplish the second stage, it is said, by the power of reflection: the chief element that makes the transition from the first to the second stage possible is mindfulness.

A crucial issue here—I can't emphasize this too strongly—is relaxation. Especially if you tend to become very goal-oriented in the practice (and I must say it practically invites goal-orientation), it is very easy, upon having found the object to grit your teeth and bear down with the resolve: "I'm going to get this continuity if it kills me!" You will get continuity, and it may indeed kill you if you go about with that muscular approach to *śamatha*. You've forgotten all about ease and relaxation, forgotten that maybe you should enjoy this practice. It's called *quiescence* for a reason.

The transition from the first to the second stage (or between any two stages on the way to *śamatha*) happens gently, gradually. It does not happen overnight, or from one day to another, but rather as a gradient. You find that, more and more frequently, real periods of continuity become the norm. The way to move from the first attentional state to the second is by sustaining the relaxation and applying a subtle degree of effort to maintaining the attention. The continuity must not be won at the expense of relaxation. If you forget that, you will waste a lot of time, and frankly, the only reason to have a meditation teacher is so you don't waste so much time.

What does the second stage feel like? It feels good. It's not blissful, certainly not continuously, though you may have a little flash of bliss once in a while. But there is a calm soothing quality to it. It's very quietly pleasant and it's not boring any more. You can do it for an hour, even two or three hours, without feeling bored. It's not terrifically high quality, and it's not intensely interesting, but it is just quietly pleasant and that's worth something.

3. Patched Placement

The third attentional state is called patched placement, for the attention is patched like a piece of clothing. It's like having a pair of blue jeans with a hole here and there, but the holes are patched and there is a lot of fabric that doesn't have holes in it. At this point, you can stay on the object by and large for thirty minutes, forty five minutes, an hour. For that length of time you completely lose touch with it or occasionally forget all about it as a result of gross excitation. But you get it back pretty quickly; you are not gone for long periods of time. The object is not perfectly clear, and you have some background chatter at least intermittently, but you don't lose your attention altogether for long

.

4. Close Placement

With the accomplishment of the fourth attentional state, close placement, your mind is imbued with a deep sense of calm and you don't lose the object any more for hours at a time. You don't lose the object not because you're holding on for dear life; rather you have too much stability for the boat to rock so far over that your attention slips off and rolls into the ocean of distraction. You have very good ballast.

Once again, you have gained this chiefly by the power of mindfulness, and at this point gross excitation is temporarily overcome. How do you develop the stability and increase the staying power of your mindfulness? Simply by doing it. It takes patience more than any special technique: you go back to it, again and again and again. It is said that, at the fourth stage, the power of mindfulness reaches its fruition and come into its full strength.[10] It is a fairly simple practice up to this point, with the one caveat that you must progress through these stages without loss of relaxation. If you find your face starting to squinch up, your muscles starting to tense or your breath becoming irregular because you're trying too hard, you will only accomplish facsimiles of these stages. They will have no foundation. They will fall apart, and you'll get exhausted in the process.

When you have reached the fourth attentional state and there is a lot of continuity in your mindfulness, you are especially prone to laxity. This is the time when introspection, the monitor of the process of meditation, becomes especially important. You need to watch very closely, though intermittently, to see whether laxity is arising. The chief task at the fourth state, as you orient yourself towards the fifth attentional state, is to get rid of gross laxity. Gross laxity occurs when the vividness of the attention fades out. The remedy is to pay closer attention. You give a little more effort to it, but too much effort will undermine your stability and cause turbulence again. It's a balancing act, and it takes trial and error to master this stage. Give it just the right amount of effort to sustain the stability and improve the vividness. Improving vividness is like focusing more and more finely with the lens of your attention: one of the characteristics of enhanced vividness is that you see greater detail. I think we in the West have a different understanding of the word "effort" than the Tibetan implies. For us effort seems to be such a gross thing, but the intention of this type of effort is to become more and more subtle.

You may find that you still have a considerable amount of mental background noise through the fourth stage. This is not like an ordinary wandering thought, but more like a split focus: you are concentrating on the breath, but you can still hear a conversation going on in your mind at the same time. It's often like overhearing somebody else's conversation in which you have no role whatsoever. Or it may take the form of imagery, a slide show or a movie that appears on the periphery of your awareness.

After some time, when you've achieved good stability, a mental image similar to a spontaneous visualization may appear in the area where you have been attending. Most commonly it takes the form of a little pearl of light, or a small mesh, or cotton ball, or spider web of light. At first it will come just occasionally, and you should not pay much attention: treat it nonchalantly. Gradually it will stabilize and become routine. When it arises regularly of its own accord whenever you sit down to your meditation, then it's time to shift the focus of your attention. You move your focus from the tactile sensations of the breath and place your attention on the image that has arisen. That naturally arisen mental image, or "sign" (*nimitta*), then remains your object up to the time you reach *śamatha*. There is no definite time when that sign will appear, but it may begin to show up occasionally as early as in the third attentional state.

5. Taming

At the transition from the fourth state to the fifth, it is particularly important not to lose stability in the move toward greater vividness, just as it was important not to lose relaxation by increasing your stability. The main emphasis of the fifth stage, called taming, is to enhance your vividness. Now you really begin to see the advantages of this attentional training, and you take delight in it. Coming into the fifth stage you are already free of gross excitation, but now your task is to overcome gross laxity. By paying closer attention to the object of meditation, you enhance the vividness of your attention, thereby achieving a greater "density" of moments of clear mindfulness directed upon the chosen object.

Some of the great commentators on this practice such as Tsongkhapa point out that laxity at this stage has been a real pitfall in the past for many Tibetan contemplatives. Lacking thorough theoretical training in this practice, they achieve this state and mistake it for *samādhi*, because they are not losing the object any more. But they remain in a state of gross laxity, devoid of the potency of vividness. If a dedicated meditator does this for ten or twelve hours a day, and for months at a time, Tsongkhapa and others report that one's intelligence wanes.[11] The long-term, karmic results are even worse. So it is important not to succumb to laxity, but to recognize it and counter it: enhance the vividness of your attention.

6. Pacification

The chief agenda going into the sixth state, called pacification, is to get rid of even subtle excitation. By the time you accomplish the sixth state, your senses are pretty much withdrawn and you have very little input, if any, from the external environment. At this point, all emotional resistance to the meditation has vanished, and the continuity of your attention is now very tightly woven.

7. Complete Pacification

Having accomplished the sixth stage, there is still room for improvement in terms of vividness and overcoming subtle laxity. When you have subtle laxity, the object is clear, but it could still be clearer: there is room to heighten the pitch of vividness. What you're looking for now is intense vividness. It's very easy to be complacent at this point, but there is still ground to be gained. When you have overcome even the most subtle laxity, you have achieved that seventh attentional state, which is called complete pacification. By now you should have moved from the tactile sensations at the nostrils and you are focusing on the mental "sign" of the breath.

You still need introspection, because what you have accomplished at this point is not immutable. Problems could still crop up here and there. Some laxity or some subtle excitation could set in on occasion. The task of introspection now is like the job of attending to a sonar scope. It may not be likely that you are going to see a blip, but if a blip comes up you've really got to see it immediately.

8. Single-Pointed Placement

When you reach the eighth state, called single-pointed placement, there is virtually no danger of any kind of laxity or excitation arising. You give a little bit of effort at the beginning of the session, and when you get started it goes effortlessly. You are cruising, and you really don't need introspection much at this point. It's very, very unlikely that any problems will arise. Your external senses at this time will be shut down; you will not hear anything. You're locked in, and you just continue with that. Log your hours. You want the mind to get accustomed to this state, creating a deeper and deeper groove.

9. Balanced Placement

By the power of familiarity with the eighth attentional state, you attain the ninth, which is called balanced placement. This is more of the same. The only difference is that in the ninth attentional state you don't need any effort at all. You slip into the meditative state and remain for hours. It's a breeze. Progress is still happening, however. You may think you're just biding time, hanging out, although it's certainly not boring. But just by abiding in this state, transformations are taking place. The energies are moving around, getting readjusted in the body. You are getting a new circuitry, in a sense.

THE ACHIEVEMENT OF ŚAMATHA

The achievement of *śamatha* entails the freedom from both gross and subtle excitation, and gross and subtle laxity. You can enter into the meditation upon your chosen object and sustain it indefinitely, free of laxity and excitation. Your mind comes to the object and the other senses shut down. You are utterly intent upon the object, but now it becomes effortless, you don't need to hold on tightly. It is effortless because you are now beyond any need for introspection, beyond the need to apply antidotes for problems. It is as effortless as a hockey puck sliding on frictionless ice. This effortlessness comes just prior to *śamatha*, but as you become more familiar with this effortless *samādhi*, then *śamatha* clicks in.

The actual attainment of *śamatha* is an event, and it will not leave you wondering whether or not it happened: it will come in like the Star Spangled Banner, at a specific time—it's that identifiable. Even though prior to that you are totally focused in the mental realm, when *śamatha* takes place you feel a radical shift in the physical body. A rush of unprecedented ecstasy arises in the body and mind. You may experience foretastes of it prior to attaining *śamatha*, but it comes on in an unprecedented fashion with actual *śamatha*. This ecstasy that saturates the entire body and mind is not very useful, but it is a clear marker. It tapers off and the mind settles into a state of very grounded, vivid effortless stability, with an echo of that bliss. The body also acquires an unprecedented quality of buoyancy and pliancy. The body and mind are now very fit for service, and the pleasure involved is not so overwhelming that it interferes. And at that point, you have attained *śamatha*.

Is achieving *śamatha* really possible? It may not be feasible for everyone, but it is generally within reach. The experience of people who did a one-year retreat in 1988 led by the Tibetan contemplative Gen Lamrimpa was very inspiring. It gives me a high degree of confidence that if we approach it very traditionally, if we attend closely to the causes and conditions, the prerequisites and the environment, that we have just as much chance of accomplishing *śamatha* now in the modern West as they had in Tibet five hundred years ago, or in India twenty-five hundred years ago. They don't say you have to do the prerequisites *and* be a genius. They just say: Do the prerequisites, set up the right environment, and here's the technique. It is pretty straightforward.

It is possible if you apply yourself to it earnestly and with perseverance. A brief stab at it does not work. So a lot depends on the individual, and how oriented one is towards it, but if I didn't believe that it was within reach, I wouldn't bother to teach it. I just don't care about things you can only talk about, things you can't practice and achieve.

Even if you never achieve *śamatha*, any progress towards that end is valuable. Moreover, any progress towards *śamatha* can also be used towards other things: for the cultivation of compassion, or for any other worthwhile venture. Creativity opens up a lot through this process. Tibetans don't have a word for creativity as such, so that was an unannounced bonus from doing this type of practice. The practice also tends to bring a very powerful integrative quality to one's understanding.

If you really want to achieve *śamatha*, there is a time-tested prescription: radically simplify your life for a period and practice in such a way that your whole life is focused on *śamatha* meditation. It's been done with success many times and people know it works. There is another approach that is not so well proven, but could be very interesting. A Tibetan lama recently said that, in principle, it's possible to attain *śamatha* even while leading an active life. But it has to be a very unusual active life. If leading an active life means that your mind is scattered among your activities, turbulent and anxious, moving compulsively to the past and future, then *śamatha* is not possible. If you could engage in action with calm and with the presence of mind to simply do what needs to be done, it is possible in principle to achieve *śamatha* in an active way of life. You would need to set aside periods throughout the day for *śamatha*, and you could not afford to let your activity become compulsive, frenetic, or agitated. As an approach, it's more risky: it has not been proven very often. But for those of you who are more adventurous, accomplishing *śamatha* in an active life would be headline news, an important breakthrough for Dharma in the modern world. Accomplishing *śamatha* even by traditional methods, in solitude, would be fantastic. I would love to see several Westerners do it, because that could bring about a major transformation.

When I first received training in a Tibetan monastery in 1973, the prospects were extremely daunting. We were about to begin learning in detail about the five sequential paths to omniscience. The first path begins when you are a *bodhisattva*; eventually you have your first unmediated experience of ultimate reality, and there are nine stages after that. We were about to embark on a six-year training program to learn in detail about those five paths and ten stages, which start from the time you have an unmediated experience of the ultimate! It was impossible for me to relate to this material experientially. I wanted a practice I could actually do.

Whatever goals one might hope to achieve, it's always good to come back to things that are within reach. Living an active way of life, the demands are sometimes heavy. I confront this a lot in my own life, and especially when I need to travel it's hard to maintain a substantial meditative practice. I like to do three or four hours per day, and it's really hard on jets and with moving around a lot. When I've been traveling a great deal, I begin to wonder if I am really getting anywhere in the meditation. But then I look at what I'm doing, and ask myself if all this activity is worthwhile. And I think, yes, these are all meaningful activities. None of it is trivial. I'm rather keen on meditation, but the bulk of my waking hours per day are not spent in formal meditation, and that time spent actively really is the platform of my life.

THE PREREQUISITES FOR ACHIEVING *ŚAMATHA*

How do we bridge the gulf between our active lives and the goal of achieving *śamatha*? Addressing the traditional prerequisites for *śamatha* is a very practical start. Even if you are not particularly interested in *śamatha*, the prerequisites are good guidelines for a meaningful grounded, balanced, and vigilant way of life.

1. A Suitable Environment

The first prerequisite is a suitable environment. This is the easiest and most mundane of the six: it merely costs money. A suitable environment is a very straightforward requirement, but upon careful inspection it also turns out to be quite unusual.

As traditionally defined (which assumes a retreat situation), a suitable environment is one that is quiet, without the sound of people talking by day or dogs barking at night, for example. It should be safe so you don't need to worry about bandits, muggers, vipers, lions, tigers, or elephants. It should be a clean and healthy environment, one where you feel comfortable. You feel at home and enjoy the place. It should not feel like an alien, let alone a hostile environment. It should be very easy to meet the basic needs for sustenance: food, clothing, and lodging. For people who are starting out as novices in the practice, it's best not to be completely isolated but it's also good not to be with a whole crowd of people. Three or four companions would be optimal. You would not necessarily be meditating in the same room but nearby. The reason for having a few companions is to lighten up, have some friendly conversation during the breaks. Deep solitude can become very heavy and it helps to balance the practice with some warmth of human companionship, a sense of comradeship. This is your Saṅgha, your community. It's very nice for your environment to have a place where you can gaze out over big horizons. That means having not just sky, but also specifically a far distant view you can focus on.

It's interesting to note that Tibet had a wonderfully high percentage of yogis: something about the environment was appropriate there. I can't help but wonder whether the high altitude helped. Some of the yogis from Tibet had a much harder time when they came down to India. But if you should think about going on retreat in Asia, you might want to think again. There are eight hundred million Indians in India, and it's very hard to find a place that's really quiet. Health is always an issue, food is an issue, visas are an issue, the cultural differences are an issue. As the yogi Gen Lamrimpa said,

"You've learned the teaching, why don't you just go back home? It's so much nicer to meditate in North America than it is here." So, it's not that easy to find a really suitable place. But it is feasible if people have the intention and can afford it. And Americans are fortunate in this: we have lots of land. I dream especially of retreats in the great, vast spaces of the Southwest.

Environment is as important to practice in an active life as it is to a retreat. For brief periods I have lived in environments where the problems were bigger than I was, and I could not flourish. I tried and I tried to rise to the challenge, but I found it so hostile, adversarial, and unsupportive, that I couldn't—that was the long and short of it. I found myself unable to control feelings of injustice and resentment. Finally I realized I did not have to stay there. Why not move? A simple shift of environment allowed a happy mind again. It may be a living environment, or an occupation. Perhaps your job is just a rotten place to be, and engaging in that kind of activity eight hours a day will tear you apart. If you are defeated it is better to shift. Of course, there are still issues to deal with, but you don't need to subject yourself to challenges beyond your capacities. The environment has a lot to do with your sense of contentment and satisfaction, and it is important to be easily satisfied.

2. Contentment

The second prerequisite is contentment. This simply means being satisfied with the given: attending to what is present, in terms of the quality of your food, clothing, lodging, and so forth, and being content with it. In other words, don't fantasize about all the things you don't have, but look at what you do have and be content with that. This is very specific and not an unreachable ideal.

3. Having Few Desires

The flip side of the coin of contentment is having few desires. Of course, you need to have some desires: if you run out of food you need to get some more. But let them be few and simple.

4. Ethical Discipline

The fourth prerequisite is pure ethical discipline. This doesn't mean you have to be a saint. "Pure" doesn't necessarily mean you have perfected ethical discipline. The ten precepts are a good framework: avoid killing, sexual misconduct, stealing, lying, slander, idle gossip, malice, avarice, and false views. Attend to these precepts and if you break them, then seek to recognize it as swiftly as possible. Recognize it as harmful, and develop a resolve not to indulge in such injurious activity in the future.

5. Having Few Concerns

The fifth prerequisite, having few concerns, really confronts the issue of whether it is possible to achieve *śamatha* in the context of an active way of life. Traditionally, the way to have few concerns would be to radically simplify your lifestyle. That's a tried and tested way. But is it possible to have a more normal life, engaged in an occupation, encountering people, and still keep the mind simple? If one can avoid having the mind compulsively concerned with a whole myriad of details and issues, then in principle it may be possible to develop *śamatha* in the context of an active way of life. At first glance it looks impossible, given my lifestyle. And yet, in my experience, the quantity of activity is not really the main issue here. There are times when I have relatively few things to do and still my mind is unbelievably cluttered with concerns, enmeshed like a fly in a spider's web. There are other times when my mind is healthy and balanced and very peaceful even though I have a lot to do. At these times the mind is simply uncluttered: it moves appropriately from one thing to another, and at the end of the day everything that needed to be done got done. In that sense, the mind never has a lot of activities; it only has one activity: what it's doing right now. When it's finished with that, then it's doing something else. But that's all it's doing. A mind like this does not have a multitude of competing activities; it is just doing what needs to be done. It's a very practical way to live.

6. Avoiding Compulsive Ideation

The sixth prerequisite is to get rid of compulsive ideation completely, especially concerning desires. Such compulsive ideation includes cravings for delicious food, for sex, wealth, fame, and so on. One retreatant described this in a delightful way. He was doing well and had found a lot of serenity in the practice, but compulsive ideation would arise in the form of goofy desires. In the midst of the retreat a spiel started to arise in his mind: "Maybe I'll be the first Westerner to attain *śamatha*. And if I do, I might get on the Johnny Carson Show!" When he told us, of course he was laughing at himself, but that's an example of one form of compulsive ideation.

I find this the hardest prerequisite of all. Getting rid of compulsive ideation completely is a pretty tall order. But so much of the mundane stuff that floods our minds all day long does not really need to be thought. What do you do about it? *Vipassanā*, or mindfulness practice, is especially helpful for this. It doesn't require the iron-clad focus or pinpoint concentration of deep *samādhi*. You do, however, need to become present in your senses, to calm the mind and bring it into the present. It's a fine practice and you can do it anywhere. You can practice while in conversation, while making food, while having a great time. It can even be done in New York City for short periods of time! This type of meditation is not the same as formal sitting. It's a more open-faced presence, open to the world. So often if we try to focus the mind, especially with eyes closed, we just get lost in rambling thoughts: going outside may be the perfect antidote. I was just sitting outside in a chair quietly watching some bees go for the flowers, and I could easily imagine doing that for an hour. But it means paying attention, not becoming bleary-eyed. In fact it means being very, very present. It's a grounded, beneficial practice. It's easy to see that if you get really good at watching bees on flowers, or watching a tree, or just walking quietly, then shifting from that to sitting quietly and being present in your body is a simple matter. And from that you can make a seamless transition to attending quietly to your breath, and proceed into the nondiscursive meditation.

When I look at my present lifestyle, I know that I don't have a lot of time for formal meditation, though I do what I can. But I can cultivate the six prerequisites in an active way of life. If one day I decide to do another traditional *śamatha* retreat, the retreat will go well to the extent that I have already cultivated those prerequisites and made them part of my life. If I still have a lot of homework to do, then I could spend a whole year in a *śamatha* retreat and achieve nothing except frustration. The six prerequisites are not discrete goals, states that you have accomplished or not. Rather, insofar as you bring them into your life, your life is made more meaningful.

FIVE OBSTRUCTIONS TO PROGRESS IN *ŚAMATHA*

The traditional teachings on *śamatha* define five obstructions, or hindrances, to progress in the practice. It is helpful to know what they are. If you suddenly have a major accident as you cruise down the road to *śamatha*, it's useful to know which brick wall you've just run into.

1. Ill Will

Ill will is the first obstacle, baggage that you cannot take with you into *śamatha*. Ill will simply cannot be sustained at the same time as you progress in the cultivation of *śamatha*. It's very possible that when you sit down to practice you'll say: "No problem; I carry no ill will, I'm happy." But when you descend into the depths of the mind, you start to stir things up like a scuba diver stirring up the mud. If there is a little bit of ill will, some old resentment lingering there, the *śamatha* may well tweak it and say: Are you alive or are you dead? And if it's alive, it will pop up and you have to clear it out. If you become absorbed in it, then you've just dropped your diver's lead belt and you are floating back up to the surface again.

It would be nice if your venture into *śamatha* were as uncomplicated as possible, so you did not repeatedly need to stop and do more homework. That's one of the advantages, one of the purposes in fact, of the loving-kindness and compassion practices: to clear the obstacles as much as possible before your *śamatha* practice.

2. Sensual Desire

The second obstacle is sensual desire. This is not to say that between sessions you should not enjoy the senses, things such as sound, fragrance, vision, the wonderful food you have or the stunning scenery. If, however, during a meditation session you start to crave these things, the craving will stop you in your tracks. I remember a five-week group retreat I did with a number of monks when I was meditating in a monastery. There was one monk in whom intense lust was somehow catalyzed by the meditation, and it was really painful for him. After all, he was a monk and was not going to act on his lust, but it stopped him in his tracks and he had a very hard time.

So, go ahead and enjoy the sensual, but recognize that fine demarcation between enjoying something when it presents itself as opposed to craving it when it's not there. One can simply enjoy a meal, and when it's finished, the meal is completely finished. If one has a sense of contentment and simplicity, that's enough. It's a matter of priorities, of orientation in one's life. If you orient your life such that sensual gratification is a priority—that happiness lies in a better hi-fi, a faster car—then that's your agenda. But that's not the agenda of *śamatha* and you can't have both simultaneously. It really is a matter of choice, but it's not a matter of tyrannical asceticism. Rather simply, if you are meditating quietly and thoughts of sensual desires come in and grab your mind, then your *śamatha* just ended. It is something that needs to be released.

3. Lethargy and Sleepiness

The third road block is lethargy and sleepiness. Again, this is not to say you should never feel lethargic or sleepy; that would be silly. But while you are meditating, if these qualities dominate the mind, then your *śamatha* has just come to an end. So sleep well. Get enough sleep before your meditation. Don't try to deal with them simultaneously, it's much better just to take a nap.

4. Excitation and Anxiety

The fourth hindrance consists of two obstacles. The first, "excitation," is a form of mental turbulence or agitation that has desire at its root. The second obstacle here has the connotation of anxiety, specifically that driven by guilt.

As in the case of sensual desires, this is a matter of priorities, of orientation in life. There are people who simply orient their life around anxiety. If good things happen, they may stop briefly; if bad things happen they get worse. There are always grounds for anxiety. It doesn't matter how much money you have in the bank, if you're afraid you won't have enough. If your life is oriented toward anxiety, the chances are extremely good that it will crop up rather dominantly in the meditation. Hopefully we can reduce this to mere episodes: "Ah, there it is! And there it goes." Clear it out or it will stop your *śamatha* practice.

5. Skepticism

The final obstacle can be translated as skepticism, but it also has the connotation of perplexity, hesitation, and uncertainty. You probably know people whose lives are oriented around uncertainty, who can't really move in any one direction. Everything is tentative, innately fearful; nothing is quite sure. Again, if that dominates one's life, it is bound to crop up in the meditation and stop it cold. It may be catalyzed through the meditation, or even focus on the practice. You find yourself wondering: "Do I have a chance at this? Is it worthwhile? Is there any point to this?" Such perplexity goes in circles; the only answer is to go back to the practice or give up altogether.

That uncertainty or skepticism is very different from another type of doubt that is enormously helpful, in fact indispensable to the spiritual path: the critical mind. Ideas present themselves that we don't automatically believe—Is there a continuity of consciousness after death? Do we really have the capacity for unlimited compassion? We hear things and test them: What's the evidence? What's the counter-evidence?

Does the theory hold together? Check it out. This type of doubt is not a hindrance at all. It is a vital part of the cultivation of wisdom and insight. If you don't have it, you have nothing but dumb faith. The kind of doubt that is a hindrance just stands there helplessly, without moving forward, saying, "Gee, I don't know. I'm not sure."

The simple answer to dealing with the five obstructions is not to orient one's life around them. Recognize them when they come up. Some we should release altogether: there is no use at all for ill will. Others we put in their place, de-emphasizing them: sensual enjoyment has a valid role to play, but there is no room for sensual craving. Not letting your life rotate around any of these five puts you in a good position to carry through with the *samatha* practice.

Now the good news. The *samatha* practice itself is very helpful for clearing out the five obstacles. The practice develops a progression of five mental qualities that are effectively antidotes to the five obstacles. They are called the five factors of meditative stabilization, and *samatha* is the access, or threshold, to genuine meditative stabilization (*dhyāna*).

THE FIVE FACTORS OF STABILIZATION

1. Applied Attention

Applied attention is very simply the conscious directing of attention, in which you sit down and say to your mind, "This is what I want to attend to: focus here." Applied attention tends to act as a direct remedy for lethargy and sleepiness. With applied attention we now have something to do other than just spacing out.

2. Close Examination

Once you have applied your attention to the object, then you can enhance it by attending more closely. This happens especially when you have some stability and can now move toward greater vividness. Attending more closely acts as an antidote for skepticism. There's no space for skepticism or uncertainty. The dominos of our moments of attention are spaced too closely. At this point you are doing only one thing: examining closely.

3. Zest

Following the close examination of the object, the next stabilization factor of zest arises. It begins by percolating up as interest: you start attending with a greater sense of interest. It's not something contrived, but rather flows right out of the process itself. The sense of interest mounts. The better your meditation proceeds, the more interesting it gets, until it evolves into zest. The zest increases until it becomes a state of ecstasy, and that acts as an antidote to ill will.

4. Joy

Out of the heightening progression from interest, to zest, to ecstasy, there arises joy—simply a sense of well-being. This joy acts as an antidote to both excitation and anxiety. It sweeps away both the desire-driven turbulence of the mind and remorseful, guilt-driven anxiety.

5. Concentration

The Buddha declared: "For one who is joyful, the mind becomes concentrated." Concentration, or *samādhi*, arises out of joy, when that joy comes not because you are thinking about something nice, not because of a pleasurable stimulus, but rather out of the balanced nature of the mind itself. And concentration finally eliminates the last remaining obstacle, sensual desire. When the mind goes into *samādhi*, sensual desire vanishes. It's not because you've become a great ascetic, but because you've found something so much better than anything sensual pleasure can offer.

So the good news is that if you can at least keep the five hindrances in abeyance so they don't intrude into the *śamatha* practice, then the practice itself will eliminate them. When *śamatha* is actually accomplished, those five obstacles are gone.

They are not necessarily eradicated forever, but like unwelcome house guests who have been sent on their way, you are free of them for the time being.

ON THE CHOICE OF AN OBJECT IN *ŚAMATHA* PRACTICE

In the Tibetan tradition, the object of meditation for *śamatha* practice is usually a visualization, for example an image of the Buddha, rather than the tactile sensations of the breath. Tibetan practice is very strong on visualization because almost all of Tibetan practice is directed towards Vajrayāna. Visualization and the creative power of imagination play a very strong role in Vajrayāna and Tibetan practice is gearing up for this right from the beginning. Breath awareness is a technique practiced more commonly in Southeast Asia, where much more emphasis is placed on mindfulness than on imagination.

One of the great advantages of breath awareness as an object for *śamatha*, as opposed to a visualization, is that it is much easier to get started. Most people need an awful lot of effort to get a visualization going. You have to create your object rather than find it. I've hardly met a Westerner who can sustain a visualization for a long period of time and not get exhausted. If you actually attain *śamatha* in a visualization practice, the stability and the vividness are enhanced to such a degree that your visualized object appears as clearly as if it were physically present. Moreover it is self-radiant, and you can maintain it effortlessly for hours on end with no physical discomfort.

Another possible object for *śamatha* meditation is the mind itself, as taught in the Mahāmudrā and Dzogchen traditions.[12] Some people find it discouraging, because the object can be very elusive and yet if one can do it, it can be very, very rewarding. You start with breath awareness, but when the mind becomes very still, you disengage your awareness from the breath and turn it right in on awareness itself. This is not the same as *vipassanā* inquiry, looking for the "I," but rather you are looking into the nature of awareness itself. Awareness is a phenomenon, an event. What are the salient characteristics of awareness that distinguish it from color, or thought, or emotion, or many other events? It must exist, otherwise, we couldn't hear anything, couldn't see anything. But what is the quality of awareness itself, as opposed to the objects of awareness, or the contents of awareness, thoughts and so forth? The qualities you look for in this type of practice are the experience of the luminosity and transparency of awareness.

Those are just words, of course, but all you can do is start with a few metaphors, because awareness is not like anything else in the universe. Gen Lamrimpa gives as perfect an analogy as I've found: Imagine a spring with a sandy bottom and water utterly pure and clear, lit by radiant sunlight. At high noon the sun beats down through the water, but there is not a thing in that water. Imagine now just a speck of dust floating in the midst of the water. That speck of dust, under those circumstances, appears very brilliantly. Awareness itself is like the pool of water: one of its features is vivid luminosity and another is transparency. The transparency is what makes it so hard to grab on to. But within that transparent domain, should anything appear, it will appear vividly. That quality of luminosity is present even when there's nothing in it, but having some content, like the speck of dust, makes it possible to see the luminosity and transparency. So, continuing the analogy, having begun with the breath awareness and coming to a relative stillness, you may toss up a thought deliberately, like tossing a speck of dust into the pool: "What is the mind?" You could ask anything. You could say: "Pass the popcorn," but then you would probably start thinking about popcorn. So the purpose of tossing up a thought like this is not to start pondering the nature of the mind, but just to direct your awareness to that thought, and note by its presence the luminosity of its environment. You can see the thought. Then it fades out, like the dust dissolving into the water, but the limpidity and luminosity remain. That takes some time, and it takes a very subtle mind to do it. But if you can do it, it will open doors.

This is still *śamatha* practice: the first step is *śamatha*, and the second step is insight. The problem is that it's so easy just to space out. When you're attending to the breath, you know what your object is, and you know when you've lost it. When you practice *śamatha* with the mind itself as your object, it's very easy to just sit there with a blank mind. Sitting with a blank mind is not the same thing as doing *śamatha* on the mind, which has an object, but it's an extremely subtle one.

If you have developed *śamatha* on one object, say the breath, and then you try to develop it on a different object, it won't be nearly as much work as if you didn't have *śamatha* in the first place. If the object you shift to is more subtle than what you first attained *śamatha* with, then there is a little bit more work to do. If you want to attend to something else that is of a comparable degree of subtlety, you will be able to do it with little or maybe no effort.

For the actual attainment of *śamatha*, it is said on good authority that *śamatha* will be achieved only if you're focusing on a mental object. If you attend to a sensory object, like music, or flowers, you may have superb concentration. But your concentration will not reach the same depth as if you're focusing on a mental object. It's for this reason that you transfer focus from the breath to the mental sign that appears as your *śamatha* practice progresses.

QUESTIONS AND RESPONSES: ON ACHIEVING *ŚAMATHA*

Question: How long does it take for a normal person to achieve *śamatha*?

Response: If I could only find a normal person, maybe I could tell you. If one is well prepared, has attended to the necessary prerequisites, and applies oneself to the practice full time, with intelligence and skill, in an environment that is conducive for this practice, then one may attain *śamatha* in about six months. Generally speaking, if you really want to achieve *śamatha*, then it's best to radically simplify your life, take out a section of time, and just do *śamatha*. They say that if you have really sharp faculties you can achieve *śamatha* in three months. Or, if you are well prepared but less capable, it might take as long as a year. Those are ballpark figures, of course. In the same vein, Atiśa mentions that if you have not attended very closely to the prerequisites, but just go off into retreat and try to do it with sheer determination then you can meditate for a thousand years and not accomplish it. So it might be worth your while to take a look at those prerequisites.

There are a lot of variables there. Sāriputra, one of the Buddha's principal disciples, attained not only *śamatha* but all four of the meditative stabilizations and the four formless absorptions in a matter of days. There is no way of predicting how long it will take from what you consciously know of yourself. Supposing someone had already become adept in this practice in a previous life, and was then born in California. Instead of being encouraged to develop *śamatha*, he or she is just taught how to play football and do math problems, and get very tangled up in a lot of other things that our society encourages us to take seriously. But nevertheless, if that person comes to the practice and engages in it skillfully, with the proper prerequisites, in a conducive environment, then it may take much less than six months.

On what evidence would I make such an outrageous claim, that someone might regain an attainment earned in a past life? Lama Zopa Rinpoche is a well known *tulku*, or incarnate lama who gained a high state of realization in his previous life. It is said that when he was a child of two or three years old, he kept toddling away from home, heading up towards a cave above the village in Nepal where his family lived. His mother would carry him back, but at the next opportunity he would head back up towards the cave. It happened so many times that his family asked a lama who was known for his intuition why this was happening. They were told that the child was trying to return to the cave where he had spent the last forty years of his previous life. So they recognized that this child was a natural born meditator. He became a monk around the age of five and received excellent training.

There are very powerful predilections in some individuals, spontaneous urgings to head for a cave. In his book *The Way of the White Clouds*, the German Lama Govinda writes about the death of his teacher Dromo Geshe Rinpoche. It's a wonderfully inspiring account. Before he passed away he told his students he would be coming back, and to look for him. Following tradition, they let a few years pass by before sending out a search party—time enough for this being to once again become embodied in a mother's womb, be born, and grow for two or three years. The general location of the search is determined by omens or clairvoyance. In this case the search party went south to Gangtok, the capital of Sikkim. The group of monks, travelling incognito as merchants, were walking down the street when a little boy just the right age saw them coming. He took one look, ran home and announced to his mother, "They've come to take me back to my monastery." The monks heard about this and came to question the child, who recognized them. When they brought the boy back to his monastery he recognized changes that had been made to the buildings. It would be no surprise for a person like this to do very well in meditation, because he or she will be catalyzing abilities that have already been well cultivated.

Question: Do you know many people here in the West who have achieved *śamatha*?

Response: No, I suspect it is very rare. But let's look at the reasons why, because if I simply told you how rare this is, you might find it depressing. Just for starters, a suitable environment is extremely difficult to find. It's really prosaic, but I speak from a lot of experience here: if you don't have a suitable environment, it's going to be really tough if not simply impossible.

Secondly, it's rare to find a qualified teacher in that suitable environment. To do it entirely on your own with a book would be extremely tough. Another reason it's rare is that hardly anybody tries. The Tibetan meditators I know are practicing *tummo* (psychic heat meditation), or Dzogchen, or

Mahāmudrā, or Lamrim meditations, but hardly any of them do *śamatha*. It's bizarre, but it's true. In Southeast Asia, they are all practicing *vipassanā*, and in the East Asian tradition, in Zen, they are also doing practices aimed at insight into the nature of reality. *Śamatha* is concerned with a separate agenda, namely to bring about attention, stability, and vividness. So in the three great branches of the Buddhist tradition, hardly anybody does *śamatha* now. In Tibet in the past, when the culture was more stable, there were a fair number of people who did it. People were doing a wide variety of meditations, and *śamatha* was one of them. Now it's very, very rare, but the Dalai Lama is encouraging monks to start tackling it again.

I don't feel comfortable saying that it's not possible any more simply because so few people are doing it. If you did find a proper environment and a suitable teacher, and got your prerequisites in shape, then maybe it wouldn't be rare at all. The experiment has yet to be done. We made a pioneering attempt at it during the one-year retreat in the Pacific Northwest in 1988. As far as I know, this was the first time such a retreat was ever done in the West. We learned a lot and our mistakes don't need to be repeated. If people really attend to the tradition, which draws on an immense wealth of experience, I think it's very feasible. That's a more useful way to think about it than thinking in terms of how many people in the West have accomplished *śamatha* so far.

Even when it is practiced, accomplishing *śamatha* is rare. One of the very common problems is that people try too hard. Both Tibetans and Westerners could learn a lot about relaxing more deeply and letting the stability arise from that relaxation. Although it is mentioned in the texts, the Tibetans sometimes do not emphasize this point, but they do emphasize tight attention, not letting your object drop for even a second. If you are coming from a very serene space, and your mind is already very spacious, then that is probably good advice. But otherwise, such attention can be a big problem. You can exhaust yourself and cause nervous fatigue, and if you push it, you can really do yourself some damage. Westerners, Americans especially, and to a lesser degree Europeans, seem much more likely to do that than Tibetans. And now even modern Asians seem to be having a harder time too.

BEYOND *SAMATHA*

At the very moment when you actually achieve *śamatha* in the practice of breath awareness, the mental sign of the breath that has been the object of meditation disappears and another, far more subtle, mental sign arises in its place. It arises from the nature of the mind itself, and it is intimately related to the breath. That newly arisen mental sign now becomes your object if you want to go beyond *śamatha* into the states known as the four meditative stabilizations. You attend to that new sign, and there are specific techniques for making the transition into the actual first stabilization and beyond. By the fourth stabilization your breath stops and the mind goes into an utterly profound, virtually limitless serenity. Beyond that, you drop that mental image and go into what is called the formless realm, a dimension of boundless space. Any sense of your body in meditation is long past at this point. Beyond that, you go into a sense of boundless consciousness, and beyond that into a sense of nothingness. Beyond that, you move into a state that is said to entail neither discernment or nondiscernment.

That's a description from the Theravāda tradition. The Tibetans come at it from a different angle. In the first place, it seems their tradition has not taken breath awareness as a vehicle all the way to *śamatha* for a long time. Many Tibetans have attained *śamatha*, but they have used visualization techniques and meditation on awareness instead. Moreover, the Tibetans have not generally been interested in attaining the stabilizations beyond *śamatha*.

In the Tibetan context, in which the emphasis is on Vajrayāna, you don't want to attain the first stabilization. There is a good reason for this. When you move beyond *śamatha* and attain the actual first stabilization, sensual desire—one of the five hindrances to achieving stabilization—is temporarily suppressed altogether. Whether the stimulus is food, music, sexual, whatever: it's like giving a lion a salad. That's all very well if you're following Theravāda practice. If you want to escape from desire, you're halfway there. Now all you have to do is practice *vipassanā* and you can cut desire right at the root.

In contrast, in Vajrayāna you don't want to totally suppress all of your sensual desires. You certainly don't want to be overwhelmed by them, but you don't want to eliminate them either. You want to be able to beckon desire at will, to elicit it for the purpose of transmuting it. This is thoroughly within formal practice. One generates a sense of bliss in the context of one's sensory experience. For example while eating, or while experiencing sound, or in sexual activity, your transmute the experience. But rather than coming to it as an unhappy beggar who seeks happiness externally in the sensory experience, in Vajrayāna practice you let the bliss that comes from a much deeper source suffuse and transmute the pleasure of ordinary sensual experience. This can be misread or trivialized in many different ways, but the point is to bring the bliss of a very, very deep state of consciousness into your sensual experience, so that it takes on a transcendent quality.

It seems that for centuries the Tibetans have not been practicing the higher meditative stabilizations. They are, however, interested in *śamatha*, which takes you to the threshold of the form realm. As long as you are right there on the threshold, you have access to desires but you aren't overwhelmed by them.

What would be the advantage of going into those other realms? It's a matter of exploration, but a purification also takes place. Theravāda Buddhism takes a pretty cut-and-dried approach towards the mind afflicted with delusion, attachment, and hostility. The goal is to totally eradicate these afflictions, sever them from the roots so they never come back again. In other words, it's all-out extermination, and the purification of the meditative stabilizations has a value in this approach.

Another approach, which is common to all Buddhist traditions, is to put the *śamatha* to use in the cultivation of insight; you have earned an absolutely superb tool for investigating the nature of reality. There is a whole array of disciplines, modes of inquiry and investigation that can optimally be used with *śamatha* and they are radically transformative. You can use them without *śamatha*, but you just can't do it as well. Or, take that extraordinarily serviceable mind and apply it to the cultivation of loving-kindness and compassion. That would be immensely worthwhile.

Chapter Four
Loving-Kindness

The word for loving-kindness in Sanskrit is *maitri*, or *metta* in Pāli, which is related to the word for "friend." A prosaic translation for this word is simply "friendliness." In English, friendliness describes a mode of behavior—a friendly way of behaving. That's certainly a component of the meaning intended here, but loving-kindness is essentially a quality of the mind, although of course it expresses itself in behavior. The essential nature of loving-kindness is a yearning that the person on whom you are focusing your mind be well and happy. We can expand on this yearning in a prayer that seems enormously rich as I reflect on it over the years:

> May you be free of enmity. May you be free of affliction.
> May you be free of anxiety. May you be well and happy.

Bear in mind that the object of one's loving-kindness may be oneself, another human being, or an animal, or any sentient being. Also, affliction may be mental or physical.

The Buddhist teachings compiled by Buddhaghosa start off the practice of loving-kindness by focusing first upon ourselves. The Buddha declared, "Whoever loves himself will never harm another."[13] Buddhaghosa's fifth-century text is

↑ not referring to
selfish love here though

strikingly pertinent in our society, because we seem to be peculiarly afflicted by low self-esteem, self-contempt, and self-denigration. It's very common, especially among Americans. It's not unheard-of in Europe, but they seem to be less subject to this type of affliction than are Americans. There are other cultures, such as the Tibetans, for whom that whole mindset seems utterly bizarre. When I was studying in a monastery in Dharamsala, one day the abbot told me, "Of course, we never think or talk about our own faults; we only talk about the faults of others." I countered that I think and talk about my faults a lot; that it was a big issue for me. He wouldn't believe me. He thought I was pulling his leg, and I could not persuade him otherwise.

At the third Mind and Life Conference in 1990, on the role of the emotions and mental states in healing, the *vipassanā* teacher Sharon Salzberg at one point addressed the Dalai Lama.[14] She explained that, when teaching the loving-kindness practice, she begins by encouraging the students to focus on themselves. First you develop loving-kindness for yourself, then for a loved one, then for a neutral person, and finally for a person you're having a hard time with. You expand outward, but you start with the self. She explained that this seemed indispensable when teaching in America because the issue of self-contempt is so very prevalent. If you skipped the first step, loving-kindness toward the self, people might maintain the position, "I'm no good, but I hope you're happy." This is not a very firm foundation. She asked His Holiness whether he felt this was a viable and worthy way to begin the practice, addressing the problems of low self-esteem among students, given that it might be misinterpreted as self-centeredness, which is antithetical to the *bodhisattva* ideal.

He looked at her as if she had just said, "All the people I teach have heads made of green cheese." He had understood the words, but he really didn't know what she was talking about. This is a man who has traveled a lot, but when he is meeting with the President, or the Senate, or environmental groups and so forth, they're working on their agendas. They don't talk about their low self-esteem. "You mean," he said, "people really don't feel they're worthy to be happy? They feel contempt for themselves?" Sharon said yes; and the whole room fell silent, because it was obvious he was dealing with a very alien topic. After talking it over a bit more, eventually he turned to the others in the room, about twenty people, many of them Westerners, and he asked how many had experienced this. Just about all the hands went up. In Tibetan culture, this is alien. Like smallpox in the Polynesias five hundred years ago, it seems they had not been subjected to this illness before.

His Holiness made a final comment that was worth noting. He asked whether, in the midst of low self-esteem people still tried to find happiness. By and large the answer is yes. People still try, even if they don't feel they are worthy of it. And so His Holiness stood by his basic premise that compassion is the fundamental emotion. We still feel compassion for ourselves; it just gets buried under a more superficial layer of low self-esteem, contempt, self-denigration, and guilt. (They don't even have a word for guilt in Tibetan!) Yet, even through all this, self-compassion still seeps up and says, "Nevertheless, I still want happiness. I still want to be free of suffering." Many hundreds of discourses on Dharma that I've heard from Tibetans have begun with the statement that every sentient being seeks happiness, and seeks to be free of suffering. Such a simple truth, yet it's worth bringing front and center. Every single sentient being wishes to be happy and free of suffering. By no means does Buddhism say this is wrong; rather, this is where we start from.

The very root of this yearning for happiness, this yearning to be free of suffering, is the fundamental expression of the *buddha*-nature. If for the time being we turn our gaze away from the myriad ways that we can stray from the agenda— trying to find happiness by buying a more luxurious car, or a bigger house, or getting a better job—and just come back to the primary desire of wishing to be happy, we find at the very source of our yearning for happiness the *buddha*-nature wanting to realize itself. It's like a seed that wants to spring into the sunlight. Sometimes it gets terribly contorted, when we want to injure somebody else for the sake of our own happiness, but the fundamental yearning is something to be embraced.

There is good reason to believe, at least intuitively if not on the basis of hard evidence, that the very nature of consciousness itself is a wellspring of loving-kindness. It is said that the very quality of the *buddha*-nature is that of inexhaustible love, and it is already there. In other words, you don't need to get it from anybody else: not from a religion, not from a teacher. It's there already, but it does get obscured. So if this is a birthright, a capacity we bring to life, then instead of emphasizing how to cultivate this wonderful quality of mind, we can shift our mindset to ask how to stop doing what we are doing to obscure it. Not: "How can I learn some really clever technique, some state-of-the-art technology for developing loving-kindness?" But rather, "How can I recognize what I'm doing to stifle the loving-kindness that is already latent within me?"

MEDITATION: LOVING-KINDNESS FOR ONESELF

The first step in cultivating loving-kindness is to spend time in discursive meditation. What we've done so far in the *śamatha* practice is nondiscursive: stabilizing the mind and bringing vividness to it. As valuable as this is, it is complemented by discursive meditation. When the Buddha said, "I visited the four quarters," he was directing his mind. Likewise we direct our own minds metaphorically to the four corners, exploring the world, our own experience, our own past, people whom we know, and others' experience. Even in a discursive meditation it helps to begin by stabilizing the mind. You can start with breath awareness. The posture is not particularly important, as long as you are comfortable and not lopsided.

The practice of loving-kindness begins with oneself. Loving-kindness in the Buddhist context entails a heartfelt yearning that the person, or sentient being, whom we bring to mind might be well and happy. Just that: be well and happy. May this person's desires and yearnings be fulfilled. May this person find happiness. There are immensely good reasons for beginning this practice directed towards ourselves, especially in the culture in which we have been raised. It may not always be appropriate, but for us it usually is.

We begin with a vision of the nature of the practice: what the point of the practice is, what it is designed to yield or bring forth. Bring to mind some image, as if this were a vision quest. It's helpful to have a vision of what human flourishing and happiness is about. What does your own human flourishing entail? How do you imagine it? Holding this vision, we bring forth a well-wishing for ourselves, that we may cultivate these qualities through the practice. May we thrive and prosper in this. May our practice yield the fruits for which it was designed, and yield our own well-being, both in solitude and in relationship to others. Let us inspire ourselves to engage in the practice so those fruits may be realized.

We might also take a baby step here towards integrating the cultivation of loving-kindness with the practice of *śamatha*, wishing upon ourselves the benefits and blessings of the *śamatha* practice. We can let the loving-kindness of that yearning for ourselves launch us into the *śamatha* practice itself. There are great blessings that can be derived from the practice of *śamatha*: the quiescence and sense of well-being that arises from the mind; the freedom of attention; the sense that the mind is serviceable, there to be used as we wish, rather than that we are being manipulated and misused by our own minds. What a blessing, to claim the mind as a fit instrument for service!

We can also continue the meditation in the discursive vein and look at the role of hatred in obscuring loving-kindness. Of course there are many things that obscure loving-kindness, but according to the Buddha's experience the number one adversary to loving-kindness is hatred. Another term for that enemy is contempt, or hatred flavored with a sense of superiority: "Not only are you despicable and unworthy of any kind of happiness or well-being, but you are totally inferior." It is as far a contrast to loving-kindness as one can possibly imagine.

Whenever hatred, malice, contempt, and disdain are present in the mind, loving-kindness will not be present. If loving-kindness is present, none of those will be present.

How does hatred influence human communities and individual lives? To the extent that we have succumbed to this affliction ourselves, how has it influenced our own lives? We can make this a thoroughly individual practice, recalling all that we know of our lives and other peoples' lives, individually, socially, globally. What are the effects of hatred? What is its nature, its quality? Just check it out. You don't have to accept any dogma here: check it out for yourself.

Then look at alternatives. Think of cases in your own life, in the lives of other people, of communities, where you can say: Yes, there was injustice, and yet people responded with forbearance, patience, and strength. They responded with courage but without aggression. Think about the relationship between hatred and fear. Forbearance and patience may not be the exact opposites of fear and anxiety but they are certainly very directly opposed. Erich Fromm said "Love is the absence of fear," and there is a lot of truth synthesized in that very short phrase.

There is nothing wimpy about forbearance. It is a very powerful quality of mind, a quality of strength and courage. And that fearless strength is the foundation for the cultivation of loving-kindness. Reflecting on this sets the stage for a powerful protection. You can dwell in it like a walled city in which loving-kindness can be safely cultivated.

The practice then moves into the realm of imagination, opening the heart to let loving-kindness flow forth in the form of four expressions: May I be free of enmity. May I be free of affliction. May I be free of anxiety. May I be well and happy.

Focus now on the first of those four: May I be free of enmity. Let's expand that: May I be free of malice, free of hatred, free of the affliction of anger and irritation, of rage and resentment. This does not imply passivity, or simply accepting all adversity and injury. It does imply a freedom from this affliction of the mind. It implies a freedom to respond to adversity with passion, with energy, with power, but without this deformation of the human spirit.

As we let this yearning flow forth, "May I be free of enmity," recall the types of situations that have in the past elicited enmity or any of the other flavors of hostility. Then moving from the power of memory to the power of your imagination, visualize how you might respond to similar situations in the present and in the future. But now you rise to them with the strength of patience and without the affliction of enmity. Bring forth all your creativity and the wisdom of your imagination as well as your memory.

In the face of adversity, when we witness an event taking place that is simply terrible, Śāntideva counsels, "If there is a remedy, then what is the use of frustration? If there is no remedy, then what is the use of frustration?"[15] When we recognize with our discerning wisdom that there is nothing we can do, then he advises us simply to recognize that, and not to trouble ourselves by being unhappy, let alone falling into rage.

You may find that you don't want to dwell on these negative aspects. Some psychologists maintain that focusing even on the absence of the negative is still getting focused on the negative. From their perspective, it's better to spend more time working on the affirmative, focusing on where you want to go rather than where you don't want to be or what you would like to be free of. I think there is value in both views. It is good not simply to dwell on enmity, anxiety, and affliction for their own sake, but bring them to mind because they are part of the reality of our experience. It is worth bringing them to mind in order to imagine, in our own experience, what it might be like to respond to adversity without enmity. What would it be like? What would it be like not to allow myself to succumb to that affliction? What would it be like to rise to the occasion with courage, with creativity, and strength?

Anxiety is such a pernicious little stinker. Even when everything is perfect—you can have a wonderful spouse, a fine job, a beautiful environment, excellent health—and still you can be totally blown away by anxiety, because maybe something will change. In fact, it will, so your anxiety is well grounded! So there are always good grounds for anxiety, and anxiety is always a disease. It's never, ever useful. It's only an affliction. What would it be like to face the possibility of danger, or adversity, or pain without any anxiety at all?

Finally: May I be well and happy. Play with your imagination, with your ingenuity and sense of vision. May I be well and happy. What does that entail? It's a phrase. We're not praying that a phrase becomes true. We're directing the mind, directing our desire. May this become true; may it be so. What is your own sense of your own flourishing? It's individual; not some formula. It's in your embodied life, your life within the context of your family, friends, colleagues, work, and environment. Given the possibility of change in all of these, what is your vision of your own flourishing? Bring that to mind.

What type of person would I be to flourish as I wish? What type of a person would I like to be? The emphasis here is subjective. Conceivably, I could be happy whether I am living in the rubble of south central Los Angeles, or in some magnificent place in the wilderness. The primary question is, what would I bring to the situation? What quality of awareness and behavior would I have if I were to flourish? How might I be well and happy?

On the one hand, we are individuals and there is continuity as we move from one environment to another, from community to community, situation to situation. On the other hand, we are also contextualized beings. I'm not just an Alan Wallace: I'm a Californian Alan Wallace, in a university, in a family. It's probably not true of most of us that we are simply victims of our environment; rather in some meaningful way we have chosen it. What would it mean for me to flourish in the very context in which I live? How might I be well and happy in this environment which I embrace and accept? How might I flourish in the present?

Even as we are in the present, we are also in motion. So it is helpful to bring some ideals into the meditation. They may be lofty ideals, even extraordinary and immeasurable ideals. They are part of the present life as well. Bring them in: May I live more and more to embody that ideal. This is also a very rich part of the loving-kindness directed towards the self.

EXTENDING THE PRACTICE OF LOVING-KINDNESS

Loving-kindness directed towards oneself is a preamble to cultivating loving-kindness for all beings. Following this, there are different ways to begin the main core of loving-kindness practice, but one tried and true way is to focus initially on a person whom you admire and love. This is not simply a dear friend, but someone who really elicits admiration and respect for the excellence of his or her life. Focus on this person and bring her vividly to mind (let's imagine it's a woman). Open your heart to this person just as you did to yourself, wishing that she might be well and happy. Bring to mind her specific desires and aspirations, and then wish her well. May her yearnings be fulfilled. May she find satisfaction. Some of these desires may be personal, while others might have a broader scope. For example, the Dalai Lama would like to turn Tibet into a peace zone, with no nuclear testing and no arms. I wish him well in this regard.

The next phase is to focus simply on a very close friend. Again, as for oneself, so for the other: may he be well and happy. Obviously, a dear friend is someone you know very well, so you probably know his desires and goals, his anxieties and the resentments he harbors. For those of you who have spouses, for those of you who have children, now is the time to attend to them with loving-kindness. What a shame it would be to spend a whole retreat developing loving-kindness and never think about those closest to you. With these in mind, progress through the fourfold yearning: May you be free of enmity, free of affliction, free of anxiety; may you be well and happy. Let your heart join with theirs.

Beyond that, the next phase of the practice is to focus on a neutral person, someone to whom you really don't give much thought one way or another. If you heard that this person had just died in an automobile accident, or that he had just won the lottery, either way your mind would basically remain unmoved. If no one falls in that category for you, that is noble and excellent. But if anyone remains in that category, then focus on such an individual. It could be the person you see every few days behind the counter at the local market. Focus on him: "As for myself, so for you. You also wish to be free of suffering. You also wish to find happiness. May you experience it. May you be well and happy." Develop that. Let the loving-kindness you felt for yourself and your friend slide over to the person towards whom you feel neutral.

Of course, at each level you work with more than one person, repeating the exercise with a number of individuals. It's a really sound approach because, by addressing the mind to individuals you avoid the cliché of generic love without any object: "I love humanity, it's people I can't stand."

There is another version of this practice in which you simply turn the mind to different directions, sending your loving-kindness to the east, south, north, and west. You imagine your awareness like a beam of light: "May all you who dwell in the south be free of enmity, free of affliction, free of anxiety. May you be well and happy." In this way you suffuse the four quarters with loving-kindness. Another way to do it, rather than orienting yourself to the cardinal directions, is to focus on all sentient beings in front, behind, and to either side of you. That's a very straightforward way to do it. It's a valuable practice, especially as a complement to the individual practice. I wonder, however, whether it might not fall into the trap of generic and disengaged "love" if practiced exclusively.

You can see that the practice of loving-kindness is very simple and needs little explanation. More can be said, of course, about dealing with those for whom we feel anything but affection. When we bring to mind people towards whom we harbor resentment, our animosity may not be cleared out in the first sweep. There may be some stuff fairly deeply embedded there, in which case we address it again, bring back more understanding, and continue working to clear it out.

THE ADVANTAGES OF A LAY PERSON IN THE PRACTICE OF LOVING-KINDNESS

One of my beloved teachers, the late Tara Rinpoche, an extremely warm person as well as a great scholar and contemplative, addressed this issue in the cultivation of loving-kindness. Having been a monk since he was a child, he had the following observations to make about a monastic route towards the cultivation of loving-kindness, as opposed to a lay route. For a monk or nun, part of the motivation for removing oneself from family and becoming homeless is to develop this sense of evenness, an impartiality to those near and far. The idea is to develop a sense of kinship equally with everyone, as opposed to favoring a family for which one has a special responsibility to protect and care for. So one viable avenue for cultivating loving-kindness with impartiality is to simply withdraw yourself from personal attachments. You remove yourself physically by going to a monastery. Then, from that place of neutrality, you develop a sense of kinship, of loving-kindness and compassion for all: for your own family, and for all other beings as well.

Tara Rinpoche was telling this to a roomful of lay people, and he said that there is also another viable avenue that works. That is, one takes a spouse, has children perhaps, and remains a lay person. In that case you now have a special obligation to your own spouse that you don't have to other men or women. You have an obligation to take care of your children with a special care and affection that you don't have for other children. In fact, if you treated your own children as you treated all other children you would probably be a rotten parent. And this path is the most appropriate for some people because, by entering into such intimate relationships with a spouse and children, there is an opportunity to draw forth loving-kindness that might otherwise not emerge at all. There are some pretty crusty monks around who never get around to loving anybody. Having been a monk myself for fourteen years and a solitary monk for quite a long time, I can tell you that when you are living alone for months and months on end, you gain a very high degree of control over your immediate environment. You know exactly how much granola is in the can. Nobody's going to surprise you by saying: "You ate up all the granola? What about me?" You know that you can turn on the heater and you don't have to think about whether anyone else is too hot at night.

There are pros and cons to both avenues. But as Tara Rinpoche said, the family situation may draw forth the affection, the warmth, the tenderness of your own heart towards your own spouse, towards your own children that might never have arisen ever before. Once it has arisen, there is a sense of warmth, of intimacy, and of deep, deep caring, so much so you might even be willing to sacrifice your life for your child. If you can feel that kind of caring for anyone, it is a boon. Once you develop a sense of kinship with your own kin, then you extend it to others, developing this kinship in a broader and broader spectrum: "You too are like my family. You too are my sister." The goal is the same, but in this approach loving-kindness and affection come before impartiality. It is partial at first, but it is something good.

LOVING-KINDNESS FOR ONE'S ENEMIES

You have probably surmised by now that the goal is to be able to direct genuine loving-kindness to a person towards whom we naturally feel hostility or hatred. This would be someone whose misfortune—the loss of a job, a sickness, or even death—would bring us a feeling of contentment or satisfaction. Conversely, if we hear that such a person has won some acclaim, or is becoming acknowledged, or is doing very, very well, the mind becomes dissatisfied. Things are not as they should be: the bad guys are winning. The Buddha addresses this, identifying seven aspects of hostility that rebound on us. He is very blunt:

> An enemy wishes thus for his enemy, 'Let him be ugly!' Why is that? An enemy does not delight in an enemy's beauty. Now this angry person is a prey to anger, ruled by anger; though well bathed, well anointed, with hair and beard trimmed and clothed in white, yet he is ugly, being a prey to anger. This is the first thing gratifying and helpful to an enemy that befalls one who is angry, whether woman or man. Furthermore, an enemy wishes thus for an enemy, 'Let him lie in pain!' ... 'Let him have no good fortune!' ... 'Let him not be wealthy!' ... 'Let him not be famous!' ... 'Let him have no friends!' ... 'Let him not on the breakup of the body, after death, reappear in a happy destiny in the heavenly world!'[16]

The Buddha follows this with an analogy:

> As a log from a pyre, burnt at both ends and fouled in the middle, serves neither for timber in the village, nor for timber in the forest, so is such a person as this I say... by repaying an angry man in kind you will be worse than the angry man and not win the battle hard to win; you will yourself do to yourself the things that help your enemy; and you will be like a pyre log.[17]

Buddhaghosa comments that when you come to that phase in the meditation, you may not feel animosity for anybody. That's great. In that case, you don't need that practice. But if you do, there is work to be done. However, the practice should follow a progression. Buddhaghosa recommends not starting with people whom you loathe. It would probably be backbreaking and very painful, and it may be hypocritical as well. Instead, start where it's easiest and most natural: towards yourself. Then develop loving-kindness for a person you admire, love, and respect. Then direct it towards a dear friend, and then towards a neutral person, before you start attending to your enemies, eliminating the attitude: "This is my enemy; this person deserves no happiness, but deserves all misfortune."

In a later phase in the practice we consciously bring to mind an individual (or it could conceivably be a group) at whose hands we have received some trauma, injury or misfortune. The purpose of the meditation is to be able to bring this into the loving-kindness as well. That can be very bumpy; it may take a lot of work. It may even take years, but it is worth doing.

One approach, when you see a blockage on your path of cultivating loving-kindness, is to recognize it, acknowledge it, and back off. Then come back and saturate the mind even more deeply in the loving-kindness, where you know you have a fertile field. If you're working with individuals, direct it to a loved one, to someone you greatly admire, and to yourself. Come back and gather some momentum, and then see if you can bring that to bear and suffuse your problem person with it.

An indispensable ingredient for spiritual maturation is the cultivation of fortitude: strength, forbearance, and patience. It is simply impossible to become enlightened without having developed much capacity in that direction. Like loving-kindness, like insight, like *śamatha*, fortitude is one more quality that needs to be brought into play. It's part of the mosaic of spiritual awakening, and it is a stretch for most of us, though you may be an exception. Just as a beggar or a needy person is an aide to the cultivation of our generosity and openheartedness—if you don't have anybody who needs you, how can you be generous?—likewise people who bring us adversity are another indispensable ingredient for awakening. They are aides to the cultivation of something we absolutely need: wisdom, forbearance, and the integration of these. In that specific sense we may even feel gratitude there. Don't push this too fast or it will lead to hypocrisy, but it is in fact a viable approach at some time. If it is not viable in the meantime, if for now you can't welcome this, simply acknowledge it and let it be.

In the cultivation of even-minded loving-kindness we may find a few little lumps left over: people, communities, or

situations where we are just not up to the task of feeling loving-kindness. Part of the mind may say: "I'm sorry, but they
don't deserve it." We think, possibly, of the injury they've inflicted upon us, or the injury they've inflicted upon somebody
else, or maybe they're just downright nasty, cruel, vicious, or
obnoxious. So what can we do? The first thing that comes to
my mind is a simple comment I once heard, a comment that
held enormous power because of its context.

Tenzin Choedak was the personal physician of the Dalai
Lama in Tibet in the late fifties. He was a monk, and an outstanding physician and healer. When the Dalai Lama fled Tibet, this man was captured by the Chinese Communists. For
about eighteen years, he was imprisoned in a concentration
camp, tortured, and given pig swill to eat. Eventually they
released him, on the death of Mao Zedong. Before long he got
out of Tibet, was able to rejoin the Dalai Lama, and was immediately reinstated as his personal physician. His comment,
which I found stunning—and I simply believe him—was that
during those eighteen years he never harbored hostility, anger or hatred towards the Chinese.

If he had felt some anger at times, or if he had felt life-
consuming rage and resentment, would that be justifiable?
From a purely mundane perspective, of course it would be.
He didn't do anything to these people, and they tortured him
for eighteen years because he had the audacity to sign a docu-
ment stating that Tibet was not part of China. If that's not
justifiable anger, I don't know what is. But if you told him
that, this monk would think you were talking gibberish. What
does that mean? Is there justifiable cancer? Is there justifiable
AIDS? Are there justifiable brain tumors? These are diseases.
Hatred is a disease, an affliction. It pains us.

There are insight techniques that are enormously useful
responses to hatred. They are antidotes to a disease. Most of
these antidotes involve using wisdom to support compassion.
When compassion, or loving-kindness, ventures forth and
meets with hindrances, it takes insight to break through those

barriers. For a person who is strong in wisdom, Buddhaghosa suggests that insight practice applied to the object of hostility can be effective in removing the barriers.

One technique is to focus on a person who arouses a response of anger or hatred. It may be a person who wishes you harm or has done you injury in the past. Buddhaghosa points out that as you succumb to hatred, you are inflicting injury upon yourself. You may or may not get around to injuring the other person, but as soon as hostility arises in the mind, you're already damaging yourself, and so in a sense you're accomplishing the task of the enemy. It's bizarre, but it's true. So focus on that.

When hostility or hatred arises, it's obsessive. It compulsively focuses on the negative qualities or behavior of an individual or a group of individuals. It does not attend to how it feels to have this affliction. Buddhaghosa suggests looking at what it feels like. How does it affect you? Recently physicians have been speaking out more and more frequently about the purely physiological effects of hatred and rage—whether suppressed or expressed—and it's all negative. It's a good way to destroy your heart, let alone what it does to your sleep, your digestion, or your mental well-being. It's just an affliction. So, if it's not overpowering, just apply that recognition and attend to it.

We come back again to William James: what you attend to becomes real for you. Anger arises, and note: there is an affliction. Hatred arises, and there is an affliction. Just recognize it and that will already start to disempower it. It's not a matter of suppression; it's just a matter of disengagement. That's one response.

Hatred tends to simplify and to turn its objects into cartoons. Hatred very rarely, if ever, engages with a real person, with all his or her complexities. Hatred is not interested in the many facets of its object, the whole contextualized history within a family and an environment. To counter this, one possibility is to turn the attention to a person towards whom one feels hatred, and examine whether there is anything other than negative qualities. Is there a glimmer of any light there at all? Focus on that, abide with it, and start to open it up. It's like a fissure in a rock. Open that up, and engage with a person instead of a cartoon.

Another way to apply wisdom is to bring awareness to how we focus resentment on an episode. On such-and-such a date, at such-and-such a place, that person did this. Whenever we recall that person, that episode comes to mind. Or maybe the mind, with all its intelligence, sifts through and recalls other episodes of the same sort. We know the person has been like this in the past, so we extrapolate the same qualities or behavior into the present and the future, until we have a homogeneous glob of disgust based on a single episode, or maybe a series of episodes.

Buddhaghosa draws our attention simply back to our own existence. And what we find in our own lives, for example through *samatha* practice, is that we are constantly in a state of flux. One moment the heart is open, and then fifteen minutes later I'm embroiled in some petty grumpiness with a totally different mind-state. You wonder how can these two attitudes even be neighbors? But they are, and they can shift rather quickly. That little grumpiness gets embarrassed and goes away, and the mind becomes wholesome again, then something else comes up. A whole flux of situations is continuously arising. Sometimes it's unwholesome, sometimes wholesome. But hostility doesn't attend to that flux. Hostility locks onto an episode or some facet of a person's disposition and then extrapolates: This person must be this way; I know that from my experience.

There's one person with whom I was once in strong disagreement. Oddly enough, we had never met personally but he attacked me in an especially obnoxious way. I was rather sensitive at the time and it hurt a lot. Hard feeling arose and then it was over. I'll probably never meet this person, but whenever I see a photograph or hear the name, just this one episode comes to mind because it's all I have to work with. I don't know if he has a girlfriend, I don't know if his parents are living. If he were truly as bad as I perceive him, his parents would have left him out on a rock at birth and forgotten about him. But he survived somehow, so there must have been something more than what I saw. It's a classic case. I don't know this person at all. All I have is a little cartoon. And it is dead certain that right now there is no referent to my notion of this person. I have an idea but there is no thing that corresponds to my idea. All I'm doing is creating a little pile of garbage in my heart, which is a waste of time at best.

Why do we hang on to such incidents? They have no redeeming value, no benefit, although sometimes we think they do. I have heard people try to defend righteous anger as justified. But with a little bit of wisdom, we can see it just doesn't make any sense. Hatred is not even rational, it's sheer obsessive compulsion. It tastes like cod liver oil going down, but it doesn't do you any good. And to move beyond it is just a matter of eroding a momentum, breaking it down in a variety of ways.

Generally speaking, you begin insight practice by trying to identify your self. You ask yourself, "Who am I? What is the referent of my sense of 'I'? Is it my body, my mind, my emotions, my feelings, my will, my desires? All of the above?" You find, of course, that there is absolutely no referent. The sense of self that we normally hold is as false as if I were to claim to be Napoleon. This false sense of self may not always be operative, but at times it is grossly present. A favorite instance of this in the Tibetan teaching is what you experience when you are falsely accused. Suppose that an acquaintance were to accuse you, in all seriousness, of having stolen his wallet. Immediately a sense of self arises, "I did not!" And the "I" at this time is as big as a target. But what is that '"I"? Not your body, and not your mind either. It has no referent whatsoever. It's not the collection of all the parts, nor is it some metaphysical substance in the background, some keyboard operator in the brain. It just doesn't exist at all.

Just as there is no referent for the '"I" that we focus on when falsely accused, similarly there is no referent for the person to whom we direct virulent hatred or animosity. In other words, we are dealing with pure fiction. This is not to say it has no basis. Delusion normally has a basis. But the basis is not the same as the delusion. The basis is only the springboard for the delusion that goes beyond reality into its own realm of fantasy.

The practice suggested uses wisdom for overcoming hatred. Focus on the person or the community towards whom you feel this hostility and then attend closely to that individual or group. What exactly is the object of your hostility? If you find, for example, that your resentment has been lingering for twenty years, that is a dead giveaway the target probably doesn't exist at all. But attend to it. Where is it? When you're angry with someone, what is it that you are angry with? Is it the body? Is it the hairs on the head that you're angry with, or any other part of the body? You go through all the possible components and examine each one. What you find is that there is no one at home.

The conclusion we are aiming at is not that there is no person. But is the person to be found in the body, or in any of the aspects of the mind—sense perceptions, emotions, intellect, will? No. Is the person to be equated with the sum total of all the aggregates? That is more debatable, but I think that careful investigation leads to the conclusion that the whole is not equivalent to the sum of all the parts. Neither the individual parts, nor the sum total of the parts is the person. Does this mean therefore, that the self doesn't exist at all? No, it does not mean that. It is still possible to meaningfully establish that Janet exists, or Christina, or Myron. This theme of "no self" that we hear so often in Buddhism does not demolish the notion of self. Rather, it challenges and seeks to eradicate a very particular concept of self, a way of perceiving the self that has no referent. And when the mind is aroused in passion, whether the passion of hostility, or the feeling that responds to false accusation, or many other types of passion, the passion is frequently accompanied by a sense of self that has no referent. Let's take a contrary case, a sense of self that does have a referent. Imagine that someone were to ask, "How many people in this room are Californians?" I am. If the answer comes with a light touch, it may be completely authentic, a perfectly justifiable sense of who I am in relation to others. What the idea of "no self" refutes is not that a Californian named Alan exists, but that he is an autonomous entity, existing separately from any type of conceptual designation, self-sufficient and independent of any relationship.

I offer this as a matter for exploration. As exploration it's fascinating, but as dogma it's boring. As exploration, if you ever again feel anger or hatred, attend to how you are viewing the object of your anger or hatred, and observe how this person appears to your mind at that time. See whether this person arises to your mind as a someone who is contextualized, multifaceted, with a history, and a great number of good qualities as well as some bad ones. See if you can sense the interdependence with your own context: how you bring your own history to your perception of that person. Watch how a whole web of interrelationships becomes apparent. And when the passion of hostility arises, see whether you are still in touch with that contextualization. In my experience, hostility needs a radical decontextualization to create a good firm target. It needs a cartoon or a one-liner: "This person is a slob." And that has no referent. It's a waste of time, a waste of energy, and it's not even as good as cod liver oil.

Buddhaghosa's final response on this issue is just so down-home: When all else fails—you've applied all your antidotes, and still you harbor some anger—see if you can arrange either to give or receive a gift from this person. Just do something nice for him, or receive something nice from him. That may start to break up some of the hardness around that person.

If sometimes you hit a hard rock in the practice, just go back. Recognize the sheer pain of the anger or hostility itself. Then recall times in your own life when the heart has been very open. All of us can recall occasions when there was a gentle space in the mind, a time when we'd happily give someone the shirt off our back, without even a sense of sacrifice. That's when the heart's really open. There's nothing goody-goody about it. One problem we have in the West is the cloying stickiness that surrounds virtue. The genuine article isn't like that at all. It's just a spacious, wholesome sense of well-being. There is a power to it, an excellence and strength. That's a fine way to be alive. Recall that quality of spaciousness, open loving-kindness, that unimpeded gentleness of heart.

THE PROBLEM OF RIGHTEOUS ANGER

As confident as I am that what I have just said is true, I also know that it is not complete. When we see something very wrong in the world, aggression and hatred may be our ill-conceived attempt to respond. We see something terrible taking place and a passion arises, but when our horizons are fairly narrow, we don't know how many options there are. Media coverage show us myriads of things that are not as they should be, and our *buddha*-nature calls forth genuinely with passion and says: Something needs to be done. But as this call percolates up through our psyche, our conditioning, our horizons, it gets twisted so it finally emerges as a scream. Of course then it just hurts and it's not a solution. From within our limited world view, we didn't know there were other options, other ways to realize this surge of energy. Hatred is terrifically powerful, but one thing more powerful is compassion. They come from the same source but hatred gets twisted and warped. And that makes it lose its power, although it may not seem that way. There are greater powers than hatred, those that emerge right out of the *buddha*-nature without any distortion. That power is fathomless.

To passively accept any evil is to condone an evil. There are two important truths here. Perhaps the best thing we can do for ourselves is to gain access to greater options. Aristotle identified a certain quality of the human spirit as *ira*, anger, which is also translated as spiritedness. It has a fiery quality to it. Aristotle said that if we squelch our *ira*, we have diminished our humanity. We have flattened out something that was of value, something important to our fullness as human beings. Aquinas, drawing on Aristotle, elaborates on this. We should not suppress all *ira*, he says, or we will succumb to apathy in the face of gross injustice.

What does aggression have to do with enlightenment? Nothing at all. It moves in the opposite direction. But it is tapping into the same source. The source of *ira* is *buddha*-nature. It's a passion, a flame that could equally express itself in compassion, or in a passionate love, or even in ferocity, but without the malignant distortion of hatred.

There is a place for ferocity in Tibetan Buddhism, but it is perhaps the most dangerous tool that a human being can pick up. I hardly need to elaborate, because there is an awful lot of ferocity in the world already, and at least ninety nine percent of the time it is misused. But it is not something we want to eradicate forever because there may be very rare times when ferocity is the most effective response for alleviating a suffering, for rectifying a disharmony, or for bringing greater well-being into the world. But ferocity is almost always misused.

In my own personal experience I doubt I can recall a single incident in my whole life when, having expressed anger, I could look back in retrospect and say that it was the optimal response. It got something done perhaps, but it wasn't optimal. Every single time, something else would have worked better. In principle I think it is possible for ferocity to be appropriate but I don't trust my own limitations here. I don't trust that my own *buddha*-nature is sufficiently expressed that I should let rage come through unimpeded when it starts to arise. Before I allow this to happen, I would like this practice of loving-kindness to have come to fruition, so that I have learned to make no distinction between friend and enemy. If I could bring loving-kindness to both friend and enemy without any barrier, I would not need to fear my own anger. But until those barriers are removed, my anger will probably do more damage than good.

PASSION AND PATIENCE IN RESPONSE TO THE SOURCES OF SUFFERING

In witnessing an evil, a passionate response is appropriate. To respond with indifference is itself an affliction. To respond with a passion is fine in principle, but the question remains: What type of passion? If the passion is hatred or aggression, then it doesn't matter at all whether it is directed towards a person or an action. It is simply an affliction, and it does devastating harm to our own mind and spirit. I know highly intelligent people who have focused very carefully on the environment, on social issues, and so forth, and it can lead to three things that tend to go together.

One is despair. What can I do about the riots in the inner city? What can I do about human rights abuses in far-off countries? What can I do about environmental disasters? What can I do about the ozone layer? The list is as long as your arm, and focusing on that can lead to disempowering despair.

Secondly, we can say: Who's perpetrating all this? By and large it's not birds. It's not chimpanzees, or dogs or cats. It's not volcanoes or hurricanes. They do some damage, but not the damage we're talking about. It's human beings, and this can generate a fierce sense of misanthropy and a wish to withdraw: "The human race sucks. Go away! I want to shift planets."

The third response is cynicism. Despair, misanthropy, and cynicism are the afflictions of the intelligent. Nowadays there seem to be many intellectuals who are brilliant in their analysis of the human condition, but who have succumbed, like a tree getting felled, to despair, cynicism, and misanthropy. That's not how I want to wind up. That is part of the problem. When people can say of me: "Look at him. He hates everybody. He's cynical and he's despairing. What a wretched person!" I then become the object of someone else's despair, misanthropy, and cynicism.

So we need to get out of the loop. I don't know all the ways, but one way is to focus on our own hearts and minds, and recognize any misanthropy or hostility directed towards any object whatsoever. Whether it's an act, or a person, a community, a race, a gender, a religion, a religious group, a political group, it doesn't make any difference. It's the subjective side of the affliction that matters, not the objective side. Let us recognize: "Here is an enemy of loving-kindness. Here is an enemy of my own well-being and happiness. Here is an enemy of my own spiritual maturation." This is Public Enemy Number One, because it will disable me in my pursuit of spiritual awakening.

Attending to the mental event itself, what is the quality of hatred, contempt, hostility, or aggression? How does it feel? We don't need any dogma here. We have our senses and we can observe for ourselves, drawing from our own experience. One aspect of this is to examine our own personal histories, and look at the most severe conflicts that we have participated in, where just being with another person, or a group of people, becomes unbearable. Was hatred an element? We can check it out for ourselves. Then expand the question to other people we know about. When we see two people split up, is hatred an element? When communities split, is hatred an element? The object is irrelevant; the hatred itself is a malformation of the human spirit.

On the negative side, it's worth recognizing an affliction as an affliction. This is judgment, but any doctor needs good judgment to recognize a virus that will kill you. Then there is a counterpart to that. Of course, we're moving here towards the cultivation of loving-kindness. But there is a foundation, like a walled city that will give protection to the cultivation of loving-kindness. This is *kṣānti*, translated sometimes as patience. The word patience, however, may have a wimpy connotation, as if you don't have the chutzpah to respond in a manly fashion. Other facets of *kṣānti* are forbearance, fortitude, and courage—the ability to meet with adversity, whether our own or others', and not to wilt or crumble. It's a strong state of mind.

The Buddha said:

> No higher rule the Buddhists say, than patience. And no
> *nirvāṇa* higher than forbearance. Patience in force, in
> strong array—it is him I call a Brahmin. No greater thing
> exists than patience.

Forbearance, or patience, is the greatest protection for spiritual practice. It is the greatest protection for your well-being and your own flourishing.

The Tibetans speak of three different aspects of patience. One is being willing at times to take on adversity. There is a certain attitude that is simply unwilling to confront any kind of adversity. If adversity pops up, this mentality just cringes and opts out: "This isn't comfortable, so I'll slip away." I'm describing a caricature, of course, but sometimes we live up to the cartoon. This quality of mind is infertile. A mind that arises with strength to face a strong situation with courage is far more productive.

Another type of forbearance expresses itself in passivity. At times, in the face of injury or insult, patience means not doing anything. Somebody makes a condescending remark, puts us down, or injures us in some way, and we don't give it a second thought, but just leave it and say, "Never mind."

A third sort of forbearance is especially important in the course of spiritual practice. Adversities will inevitably arise in the practice itself. It's not because you're practicing incorrectly, but because you are catalyzing difficulties and bringing them out in the open. It's as if you were tilling the soil in a garden because you want to grow your vegetables or flowers. Naturally, you uncover some rocks. If you hadn't tilled, the rocks would just sit there: you wouldn't have to face them, but you'd never have any vegetables or flowers either. Dealing with the rocks is part of good tilling. Dharma practice is like tilling the soil. *Śamatha* especially will bring up some rocks that are not always pleasant. You work through them and move on.

Of course there are times when, in the face of injury, a response beyond acceptance, beyond saying "never mind," is appropriate, cases where we recognize that something needs to be done. And there are also times when it's better for all concerned if we can say, "It doesn't matter," and let it go. How can we tell when patience is the appropriate response and not just an invitation to co-dependence and abuse? Śāntideva offers a very useful rule of thumb. In his chapter on patience, he speaks of dealing with adversity as a situation that arouses a passionate response, and his answer is: Insofar as you see that your passion, your powerful urge to respond, is afflictive or aggressive, then be still until that subjective surge has subsided. Don't forget about the object: letting it go doesn't mean a response is not required. It simply doesn't need to be an afflictive response. As we know, such a response almost always makes things worse. But a wonderful thing about the mind is that it does not remain afflicted forever. So attend to the situation, and when your mind is no longer afflicted, its wholesome and naturally more powerful qualities are at your disposal. That's the time to engage, and then you can do so with passion.

When we see something terrible taking place, the situation needs the best from us. Our anger, our hurt, our despair and frustration are not what is needed. If a situation demands a response, first get your mind in superb shape, and then come back with all guns blazing. But these are Dharma guns, no violence involved.

FINDING A LOVABLE QUALITY

In his closing discussion on loving-kindness, Buddhaghosa asks: "What is the proximate cause of loving-kindness?" The answer is the observation of lovableness in the person to whom you are attending. Bring to mind right now someone whom you find lovable. It could be a person you have a romance with, or a child, or a dear friend, or a great teacher—someone to whom your heart would leap like a deer in the forest if this person were to walk through the door, someone whose presence is so lovable that a gladness arises on seeing him or her. If you can sense that in a dear friend, then try to seek out the lovableness of a neutral person. Then, finally, when you break down all the barriers, see it in a person who has done you injury.

It's a great key if you can seek out something to love, even in the enemy. Bear clearly in mind that this does not endorse or embrace evil. The crucial point here is to be able to slice through like a very skilled surgeon, recognizing vicious behavior that we would love to see annihilated as separate from the person who is participating in it. The doctor can be optimistic. A cure is possible: the person is not equivalent to the action or the disposition. Moreover there is something there that we can hold in affection, with warmth. That really seems to be a master key that can break down the final barrier and complete the practice.

One way of approaching this is to look at the person you hold in contempt, and try to find any quality he might share with someone you deeply admire and respect. Is there anything at all noble to be seen, anything that would be akin to what a truly great spiritual being would display? Focus on that: There is something there that you can love. The rest is chaff, that hopefully will be blown away quickly, to everyone's benefit. It is as if you could see a little ray of light from within, knowing that its source is much deeper than the despicable qualities on the outside. That light is what you attend to.

Again, what we attend to becomes our reality. It's so manifestly true in this type of practice. If I make a point of focusing on somebody's negative qualities, it makes no difference how good that person is. I might have to sift through a hundred stories, but eventually I could find something negative about anyone. And if I attended to that one negative story, ignoring the hundred other stories that are noble, gradually that person will appear to my mind as basically negative.

I do not encourage you here to be naive. Recognize the negative where it is present, but recognize that a person is not identical to those negative qualities or behavior. Seek out the good, and attend to that. Moreover, attending to that which is excellent and wholesome in a person often serves to draw that quality out. Skilled parents will recognize this (and to be a skillful parent strikes me as a monumental achievement). If a parent continually attends to the negative, a child knows exactly how he or she is identified. We formulate our own sense of self-identity in relationship to how other people respond to us. If we are getting hammered by our parents, friends, and teachers for being problematic, the chances are very good that we will start to create our own sense of self-identity as sleazy, or bad, or unworthy.

What do we attend to in our own lives? How do we conceive of ourselves? What do we consider to be important? When we think back on our lives, what events of our own behavior, in relation to others or in solitude, stand out as our history? A selection process takes place because we can't emphasize everything. What we emphasize becomes our reality. Learning to control the attention really turns out to have phenomenal implications. Working with loving-kindness for an enemy, we start to experience the subtlety of this and not just repeat the time-worn patterns of focusing on the negative.

CONFUSING ATTACHMENT WITH LOVING-KINDNESS

In the traditional Buddhist accounts of this practice, there is reference to the near enemy as well as the far enemy of loving-kindness. The far enemy, the extreme antagonist, is enmity or hatred. The near enemy occurs when an affectionate emotion gets derailed and turns into something that looks superficially like loving-kindness but is actually quite different. This near enemy is desire, or attachment. Loving-kindness is concerned with other subjects, other sentient beings who like ourselves yearn for happiness and wish to be free of suffering. The mental distortion of attachment is not really concerned with other people's well-being at all. It looks upon desirable objects and says: I want that, because I want to be happy. A man may look at a woman and say, "I love you," when what he means is: "I find you very attractive, come over and give me some pleasure." It has nothing to do with her well-being at all although, oddly enough, in English the same word is used. "I love ice cream." Give me some pleasure: get into my mouth. It's very clear how loving-kindness can go awry when you consider that its proximate cause is seeing a lovable quality in a person you are attending to. That's what makes us fall in love or makes us form these bonds of attachment. It's not to say that it is terrible, it's simply not loving-kindness. And it would be good not to confuse the two.

Because of this near enemy, Buddhaghosa says that it is better not to focus the practice on a person of the opposite sex (assuming one is heterosexual), especially someone that you find attractive. Particularly when you are beginning the cultivation of loving-kindness, it is not a good idea because it is an invitation to desire.

All said, it is wise to proceed slowly in dealing with the near enemy. If we love someone, in a romantic relationship for example, we may inject some false sense of this person, some reification, into our love and affection. Instead of reducing that person to something intrinsically disgusting, we see him or her as something intrinsically adorable, or lovable, or attractive. We can burden even affection with a certain type of ignorance. Does this mean that we should operate like military scouts, searching and destroying that delusion? Don't be too quick or you might throw out the baby with the bath water. Even as we acknowledge that loving-kindness and empathetic joy may be coupled with a certain element of delusion that reifies the objects of the love, it is better to proceed step by step. True, there is more work to be done, but in the big picture even this love is moving in the right direction. As you go deeper, and you conjoin the loving-kindness with wisdom and insight, then the two start to refine each other. Eventually you will remove the delusive element from the loving-kindness. Then it really is not only unconditional, but even a transcendent type of loving-kindness and compassion. In Tibetan this is called "compassion without an object." That is said to be the ultimate in compassion. But to get there you cannot always be on guard from the beginning against reifying the object of your affection.

QUESTIONS AND RESPONSES: ENEMIES
AND INSIGHT

Question: In the meditation, when I was able to feel love toward a dear friend, I felt it also returning to me. But when I opened myself to a so-called enemy, then I didn't feel anything coming back. It felt different altogether. Even though I thought I had opened my heart, it felt like there was a hidden wall.

Response: What you're saying is a fairly universal component of our experience. But loving-kindness, when it has really broken down all barriers, is sent out with no expectation of anything coming back. It would seem reasonable to expect that, as we progress towards enlightenment and gradually sift out the hostility, aggression, and pettiness of our minds, that people will like us more and more. To some extent that is true, but sometimes it just doesn't turn out that way. A classical instance of this occurred in the life of the Buddha. He had a cousin named Devadatta who became consumed with jealousy towards the Buddha. Whenever people would come to the Buddha for teaching or would praise him, Devadatta could not bear it. Until his death he held a deep malevolence against the Buddha. He tried several times to kill him, and tried to get him to step down from being the head of the Saṅgha. So it's not true that everybody will like us, or send us back love in return, even when we are fully enlightened. Don't expect it.

Question: Where does jealousy fit into the picture?

Response: Jealousy is a wicked little mutant, a very confused mental distortion. Hostility is pretty straightforward. It's basically deluded, and there's nothing strange about that. Even attachment is straightforward. But jealousy is a weird mixture of hostility and attachment together. Jealousy attends to something good, and says with malice and hostility "I can't stand that you have this—" and then adds, with attachment,

"—and I want it." Jealousy punches with one hand and pulls with the other simultaneously. Why it is bizarre is that it doesn't work at all. My feeling jealous of your fantastic little car doesn't separate you from your car or bring it to me. It's ineffective, and the only result is that I feel lousy. There's no end to these bizarre afflictions, but you start to remove them by recognizing: "This sure is an affliction. It certainly feels rotten." You begin by removing any possibility of affirmation.

Question: The biggest block to raising self-esteem appears to be judgment and self-criticism rather than contempt or hatred. Most of us seem to be much more critical of ourselves than of others. Would you classify self-criticism as an enemy of loving-kindness?

Response: It can be, but that is an area where some subtlety is necessary. When you speak about hatred there is no subtlety at all; it is such a terrible affliction. Judgment, however, is a term that may be used positively, as when we exercise sound judgment. In the *vipassanā* tradition there is a mode of practice in which you simply observe whatever comes up, without any type of judgment whatsoever. There is value in that, and there is also a value in exercising wise judgment.

Here's the catch. What we in America tend to do with judgment is to judge ourselves harshly. Our judgment is directed towards ourselves as individuals who are inferior and unworthy. This is neither useful nor wise. It's an obscurant. We turn ourselves into caricatures. A cartoon takes just one facet and presents it as the person. We should know better: that type of judgment expresses a lack of wisdom. We have a wealth of experience and a wealth of nuances, variations of who we are and modes of being that we display, but the cartoon renders them all insignificant. That type of judgment is not wisdom; deluded judgment is an expression of ignorance.

On the other hand, there is a mode of judgment that does not judge the self, but rather is concerned with recognizing wholesome and unwholesome states of mind. It's like a chef in the kitchen, throwing out junk food or anything with too many preservatives, and keeping what is wholesome, bearing in mind that what we eat makes a difference. Similarly, we digest and assimilate all of our thoughts and our mental states, and they become part of our conditioning. There are mental states and impulses that are terribly detrimental, and in meditation we can learn to recognize them as they arise. You could be sitting quite calmly eating your breakfast, when an impulse of hatred, or ill will, or contempt arises. Just like a scuba diver watching a bubble rise, you watch it come up. Then it may pop; or you may go along for the ride and develop it. Then it becomes more like oil on paper, and starts to suffuse your mentality, in which case you have to live with it for a while.

Judgment as an expression of wisdom is not in the business of judging the self. It is in the business of recognizing what are wholesome and unwholesome mental factors. When ill will arises, wise judgment recognizes it: "Aha! I've heard of you! You are the worst affliction I can suffer from. You completely destroy all loving-kindness. You're the enemy of my happiness, the enemy of my relations with other people. If I go along with you, you'll destroy all my happiness and all my friendships and I'll make myself a thoroughly miserable person. I recognize you..." That is wisdom and sound judgment too.

Question: You mentioned that the self is not the sum total, or the configuration, of all the parts. Can you explain this?

Response: The whole is certainly not equivalent to any one of the parts, but it is not simply the sum total of the parts either. All of us can be quickly persuaded that none of the parts of our self is equivalent to our self. That's pretty straightforward. On the other hand, if you walk into a room, and someone says, "You look fantastic," you may at that moment identify with your body, which is only a component of the whole.

I've also heard very intelligent people equate the self with the whole of their personal history—everything they've ever thought, all their desires, memories, imagination, body, and behavior. This is a fairly sophisticated way of equating the self with the sum total of the parts. The total is, of course, always changing and getting bigger.

One could further refine the argument by taking into account the interrelationship among the parts as yet another component of the whole. After all, we are not just a chaotic assortment of aggregates without any organizing principle. Further, we can consider what the parameters or boundaries of the sum total might be, and whether those boundaries are a mental designation. Are they culturally conditioned, or do we draw them from reality itself? Are they like the lines on a map, which don't appear in aerial photography? Can we passively witness, without any participation at all, what constitutes our self and what is other?

A line of argument may simply provide us with a comfortable philosophical position that we can then ignore in our daily lives. Now I know who I am. I've just got some philosophical baggage to carry around, without changing anything at all. But the Buddhist teachings have a way of drawing our attention to direct experience which is enormously valuable. Instead of philosophizing, we can attend from moment to moment throughout the day as we interact with other people, as we meditate, as we eat and engage in various activities—just observing, inspecting, examining as carefully and clearly as possible, how I conceive of myself from moment to moment. Who do I think I am?

We may find, again, that the mind fluctuates. Your consciousness is like a government that gets overthrown, with one coup following another over and over again. Loving-kindness takes over, and says: I'm in charge here. Then it weakens a little bit and hunger charges in: I'll get back to loving-kindness after my lunch. Sometimes these mental factors team up. For example, spitefulness, pettiness, and anger form a clique that takes over temporarily. Then they get ousted, and something else replaces them. There's an ongoing shift, a power flux in the mind. The mind is not homogeneous, not the same thing from one moment to the next.

There is a tremendous amount of fluctuation in this continuum of consciousness, and also in our behavior and the situations in which we interact. We may find that at times our sense of self, not philosophically but in actual experience, is associated almost entirely with the body. For example if somebody pushes us physically, and we react: Don't push me! All that's been pushed is the body; nobody can ever push your mind around. If our intelligence or the quality of our work is insulted, we may respond as if we ourselves have been attacked, whether defensively or wilting in depression. Or we may identify with an emotion, a particular virtue, an action, even a situation in which we were a dominant participant.

Exploring in this way, we find that in any real life situation, the referent of what we mean by "self" is never the sum total of the parts, the whole history of our experience. It's always something much narrower. At any given time, we are grasping onto a small part. In this context, the relationship of the parts, or the organizing principle, is not in the foreground. It is certainly present, but experientially I wouldn't know an organizing principle if one came and whacked me on the nose. It's there, but that's not what I'm identifying with.

It may be that nothing we ever identify with is really the self. The self is something we designate, and our sense of self can rest on the basis of any of the components of our being. If someone says to me, "Alan, you're one of the tallest people here," I affirm that, and my sense of self arises: "Yes, I'm tall." Obviously, my intellect and my passions are not tall, nor is my organizing principle, and I know that my body is not me. I can analytically probe this, and it falls apart. But still, it's true that I'm tall and I experience the identification. Examining this with a very light touch, we can begin to see that, for anything we can put a finger on to label or identify, there are processes of interdependence, relationship, and designation involved. But designation itself is a reality-maker, and not simply a reality-observer.

THE ATTAINMENT OF *ŚAMATHA* IN LOVING-KINDNESS

Just as it's possible to attain *śamatha* on the breath or on a visualized object, you can also attain *śamatha* in loving-kindness. *Śamatha* is a very specific quality of awareness, imbued with stability and vividness, which may have any of a wide variety of topics as its object. And it is possible to achieve this very fine degree of stability and vividness in the mode of loving-kindness.

How do you achieve *śamatha* in a discursive meditation? It starts out discursively, but it becomes nondiscursive. Bear in mind what the purpose is of the concepts we raise in discursive meditation. We bring thoughts to the mind in the form of words or images: May you be well and happy. But loving-kindness is not an effulgence that gushes out of the thought itself. If loving-kindness doesn't come from the thoughts, then why have the thoughts? The thoughts that we bring forth in the meditation catalyze something that is much deeper than thought. We know how well thoughts and attitudes, states of mind, can obscure or suppress the loving-kindness within and make us emotionally numb, like laying concrete over our innate goodness. But just as thoughts can obscure, so can another thought act as a jackhammer to open up what has been covered with concrete. That is why we use the thoughts. They are not designed to create loving-kindness; they can't possibly. But they can open up the heart to that which is already present, and let it flow forth into consciousness. Another way to think of it is that the thoughts are a template: they are the right shape, and we use them to create a space for something else to come up from an entirely different dimension of the human spirit.

Discursive meditation, using thoughts, words, or images, is designed to open a door, but when the heart opens in loving-kindness, then the discursive technique may become an impediment. When it starts to get in the way, you release the technique and rest in nondiscursive awareness. Just abide there quietly. There is an art to balancing this, but it is in that stabilizing, nondiscursive loving-kindness meditation that the mind really starts to shift its axis and a radical transformation can take place. This is where *śamatha* becomes melded with loving-kindness, and can really go to a great depth. That's when we really break down the barriers in the cultivation of loving-kindness.

As you develop a greater momentum in the practice, you will find that those periods of nondiscursive meditation last longer and longer. It is one aspect of the practice that will qualitatively shift, and you'll have less and less the sense that you are "doing a Buddhist practice," and more of the feeling that you are simply opening to your own inner goodness.

One way to progress towards *śamatha* in loving-kindness is to go beyond individuals. When you have spent some time attending to individuals, focusing on the enemy, breaking down the boundaries that separate your responses to various individuals, then you can place more emphasis on the latter stage of the meditation. Here the mind reaches out "to the four quarters" in all directions, enveloping all sentient beings. May we all be well and happy, without exception. As that thought arises, it catalyzes loving-kindness itself. Now it is no longer a *thought* of loving-kindness, it is the actual *experience* of loving-kindness. Once that is present, it is possible to sustain it. And that is what you do: just sustain it. Your object is all sentient beings, and you are attending to that object in a mode of loving-kindness.

It is important to recognize that the object is not the feeling of loving-kindness itself, but the sentient beings to whom your awareness is directed. You sustain that, you rest in it, and then, if you find that your attention starts to waver, then you bring in a bit of discursive thought, just enough to place the mind and stabilize it once again. If you find that the mind becomes lax, just as in other *śamatha* practice you bring in more light, a bit more clarity and vividness, and you stabilize that. This is how you actually progress all the way to *śamatha*.

If one actually achieves *śamatha* in loving-kindness, it will most likely be in this universally directed practice. It's also said that to achieve *śamatha* in loving-kindness focused on an individual, you should focus on a person who is alive. Buddhaghosa says you won't achieve *śamatha* if you focus on a dead person. Likewise, it's not possible to achieve *śamatha* in loving-kindness focused upon yourself. It's certainly worth doing, and it is a foundation of the practice, but you won't achieve *śamatha* with it. *Śamatha* in loving-kindness must be directed towards another person, or community, or a group of sentient beings.

The achievement of *śamatha* in loving-kindness takes place simultaneously "when the barriers have been broken down." The barriers are the divisions between the people I like, the people towards whom I am neutral, and the people I don't like—in other words, the distinctions I make between the people I want to be happy, those I don't care about, and those I would like to see hit by a truck. *Śamatha* is developed when those barriers have been completely flattened.

A test of this is given as a thought experiment in the *sūtras*: Imagine that you are with three people, one of your dearest friends, someone whom you have just casually met, and someone against whom you harbor the deepest resentment. A person comes along and says to you, "I am going to kill one of you, and you choose which one." Obviously, if you choose your enemy you haven't broken down the barriers. More interestingly, Buddaghosa says if you offer yourself you still haven't broken down the barriers. That would imply that you care about the others, but the field is still not level. If all barriers were down you would give no response, because there would be no preference. Your choice is no choice: "I'm not going to play this game." When you have reached this point, you will have achieved *śamatha* in loving-kindness.

Buddhaghosa describes the personal benefits of achieving *śamatha* in loving-kindness.[18] I will share them with you, not in the spirit of dangling a carrot; but rather in recognition that the benefits are felt not only by the one in a million who achieves the final goal, but to varying extents, by anyone who makes any progress at all in the practice.

Among the benefits of breaking down all the barriers the Buddha declares, "Herein, one sleeps in comfort." Instead of sleeping uncomfortably, tossing and turning and snoring, one falls asleep as if one were going into a deep meditation. So, loving-kindness is an antidote for insomnia. Secondly, "one wakes in comfort." Instead of waking uncomfortably, groaning and yawning and turning over, one wakes without contortions, like a lotus opening. Moreover, "one dreams no evil dreams." One sees only auspicious dreams, "as though one were worshipping a shrine, as though making an offering, as though one were hearing the Dharma. One does not see evil dreams as others do, as though surrounded by bandits, as though being threatened by wild beasts, or falling into chasms." The fourth benefit is that "one is dear to human beings," as dear and beloved "as a necklace worn to hang on the chest, as a wreath adorning the head."

One is also "dear to nonhuman beings." According to every culture apart from ours, our planet is richly populated by nonanimal, nonhuman beings. We're the only people who think humans and animals are the only sentient beings on earth. Everybody else believes that there is a much richer population, including such beings as *devas* and *nāgas*, tree spirits, land spirits, mountain spirits, and a variety of other creatures. There is nothing supernatural about them, but they are our neighbors.

"Fire, poison, and weapons do not affect one" who has attained *śamatha* in loving-kindness. I have heard this from many other Tibetan sources as well, that there is an extraordinary power in loving-kindness that has actual physical ramifications. The story of Milarepa and the huntsman is exemplary: Milarepa was meditating in a cave, high in the mountains of Southern Tibet. (He lived in many caves, some of which you can still visit, because he didn't want to get attached to one.) A hunter was chasing a deer with his hunting dog, and Milarepa heard them. The dog was yowling away, and the deer was running for its life, with the hunter in hot pursuit, shooting arrows from his bow. Milarepa immediately went into meditation on loving-kindness, and he directed his extraordinary loving-kindness down to the deer, which ran right to him and lay down panting, virtually exhausted to death. And of course, the dog came next, hot for the chase. Milarepa sits there and sends the dog loving-kindness. The dog trots up the hill, and lies down next to the deer. Finally the hunter comes and sees this skinny man dressed in a little cotton cloth up on the side of a mountain, with his dog and his deer resting together. He is very irritated so he takes an arrow, and tries to shoot Milarepa. The arrow veers off and misses wide. Milarepa is practicing loving-kindness, and the arrows are changing their trajectory in mid-air. Had Newton been observing this, maybe he would have gone back to the drawing board. Finally, Milarepa meditates on loving-kindness for the hunter, who kneels down and asks Milarepa to give him teachings.

The next benefit is very pertinent to the cultivation of *śamatha* altogether: "One's mind is easily concentrated." It is very easy to enter into deep *samādhi* of any other sort that you wish. The mind of one who abides in loving-kindness is quickly concentrated, and there is no sluggishness about it. Next, "the expression of one's face is serene... like a palmyra fruit loosed from its stem." Further, "one dies unconfused." One passes away undeluded as if falling asleep. Finally, "when one passes away from this life, one reappears in a Brahmā world, as one who wakes from sleep." This is a *deva* world, a celestial world of beings of light.

The Dalai Lama is encouraging his monks to develop *śamatha*. Of course there are many traditional reasons to do this, but the reason that he most often emphasizes is really practical: To the extent that we can develop *śamatha*, this makes the mind serviceable for the cultivation of loving-kindness and compassion. It becomes serviceable for *bodhicitta*, the aspiration for highest awakening for the benefit of all creatures. As you go further in the practice, it becomes evident why that would be the case. As you tap into a deeper sense of well-being, of serenity within, then it's simply easier to extend loving-kindness to others. Whereas if your mind is fraught with anxiety, or just clamped onto your own issues, it's very difficult. *Śamatha* gives you some freedom, some space, and it is a very fertile platform on which to cultivate deeper loving-kindness.

Chapter Five
Compassion

The Sanskrit term *karuṇā* is normally translated as *compassion*, but etymologically it simply means *kindness*. If I have a sense of kindness towards you, I don't want you to suffer. It implies caring tremendously about the suffering of others, as if it were one's own.

Just as loving-kindness is the heart that longs for the well-being of oneself and others, the nature of compassion is simply the heartfelt yearning: "May we all be free of suffering and the sources of suffering." Compassion directed towards oneself is the wish: "May I be free of suffering and the sources of suffering." Compassion is perfectly complementary to loving-kindness. They fit together like a yin and yang symbol. For loving-kindness to exist, you must have compassion, and vice versa. When you experience loving-kindness as you yearn, "May you be free of affliction," compassion is already there. Loving-kindness that doesn't have that seed of compassion is ungrounded. But the flavor of compassion is different from loving-kindness, because it focuses on sentient beings who are suffering rather than on sentient beings finding joy.

The difference between loving-kindness and compassion is very simple and straightforward. Loving-kindness, in a sense, is dealing with potential. Loving-kindness has a vision. It's not simply reporting on appearances. It is indeed attending to reality, but with a vision of the potential that is possible: may you be well and happy, even if right now you're not. May it be so because you have the potential. Loving-kindness brings this to life in your imagination. It attends to people experiencing well-being and the source of well-being.

However much we may long for another person's happiness, the like of which that person has never experienced, sometimes people seem to turn into little human sow bugs. They roll into a contorted ball and suffer, with a very limited view and distorted emotions. Loving-kindness imagines how people might unfold like a lotus and experience happiness that transcends anything they have experienced in the past. Loving-kindness sees more than it witnesses.

Compassion witnesses an individual in suffering, human or otherwise. Recognizing the suffering leads to the yearning for that individual to be free of that suffering. There is still a vision; compassion focuses on the fact that one doesn't need to suffer in that way. It is possible to find serenity, equanimity, tranquillity, and the equilibrium of freedom. Compassion wishes: May you be free of suffering and the source of suffering. It observes the suffering and the sources of suffering that are present, and it holds forth the vision that this suffering is not indelibly interwoven into your existence. You have the potential to be free. May you be free.

Very simply stated, loving-kindness focuses on the positive side. Compassion addresses the negative side.

We looked at the near and far enemies of loving-kindness: desire and enmity. There are also near and far enemies of compassion. Grief is the near enemy of compassion. When compassion goes awry, it succumbs to grief. Grief has a heavy quality to it, unlike sadness which may be fleeting. There is so much in the world that calls for our compassion, that if it goes awry, an ongoing state of grief can settle in. It may look like compassion, but it's a near enemy. It's not malevolent or evil, but simply a mental burden. You might think this is compassion, caring so much for those who are in misery, but in fact what has happened is that grief has disabled you. You have fallen into a dark bottomless ocean. The object of your grief becomes your only reality, all-consuming and overwhelming. There is hardly a fissure in your attention to it, hardly any light left over, and it is utterly disempowering.

His Holiness the Dalai Lama has had many chances to deal with that kind of grief, and he addresses it like a warrior. You must deal with adversity, he says, but absolutely do not fall into despair. That's the worst you can do. Then the battle has been lost; you're finished. There he is, responsible to six million Tibetans whose country is occupied by an alien people, yet he's said all along: We're going back. Tibet will be free, and never you doubt it. It doesn't matter what the odds are, just don't despair.

The far enemy of compassion is cruelty. Just as enmity is the thought, "May you experience no happiness," so cruelty wishes, "May you really suffer." It's so obvious it hardly needs to be said, that if that yearning is present in the mind, it's utterly impossible for compassion to be present at the same time. And the reverse is also true, if compassion is present, cruelty will be impossible.

Cruelty is a deeply deluded state of mind. Probably all of us have, at least for moments, experienced cruelty: really wanting to see somebody else suffer. It need not be as extreme as the feeling, "I hope you get exterminated," but just, "I hope you suffer." It may be vast, or it may be fairly limited, but it is obvious, if we pay attention at all, that the mind-state of cruelty is immediately painful whenever it arises. There is no happiness in it at all. People who professionally torture others tend to dehumanize their victims and justify their own actions as being for the greater good. They somehow contort their world view so they believe they are in fact doing something good, and they can operate then without impediment. It's terribly hard, if not impossible, to dehumanize another person without dehumanizing yourself. I remember the story of one person in a Nazi death camp who was in charge of making sure everybody filed in line towards the showers. He would become irritated when they were disorderly, and complain, "Why do you bring these problems into my life?"

How do you respond when you attend, without blinking, to suffering and sheer evil? Rage arises easily, but you can see that it contorts your own spirit. Is there any way not to turn away, and not to become contorted? Does compassion not entail empathy? If you are empathizing with a people who have suffered unimaginable atrocities, aren't you bound to be totally consumed and disabled by grief? If to empathize with a friend's headache is to commiserate and share the feeling, then is it not the same on a broader level?

To try to get a handle on this, I go back to my own experience. Both loving-kindness and compassion require that we first develop loving-kindness and compassion towards ourselves. A heartfelt, warm, and embracing acceptance of our own existence must replace any feelings of self-denigration or self-contempt. We must allow ourselves to yearn for our own well-being and happiness, our own freedom from suffering, our own enlightenment. In our own case, what would be an ideal response to illness or the loss of a loved one? Ideally, we would rise to the occasion and transform the adversity into an opportunity for greater happiness. We would use the adversity to deepen our own wisdom and compassion, and transform it into something we can embrace. We would chew it up, swallow, and digest it, and be closer to enlightenment as a result. That's the ideal, as the Tibetans say: transform adversity into spiritual growth.

Let's say somebody crashes into my car. That's adversity. Optimally, I would like to feel no pain at all. I have to deal with the situation, but any mental distress is worthless. It's not going to do me or the car any good. As Śāntideva said: There it is. It's called adversity. Can you do something about it? If so, great. Do it and dispense with the unnecessary burden of sadness. You don't need it and it doesn't serve any function at all. Just do what needs to be done. If there's nothing that can be done for the time being, then why bother being sad? That's a tall order, of course, but it's an ideal I embrace.

To respond without sadness does not mean to respond with indifference or apathy. If it's a worthy ideal to respond to our own adversity with wisdom, compassion, courage, and strength, then we ourselves are the model for how we may respond for others. Without succumbing to sadness, transforming what needs to be transformed, and accepting with equanimity what we are not yet able to transform—if that's a worthy ideal for oneself, then the ideal for responding to another person's adversity would be the same.

When we first witness others in suffering, it is perfectly appropriate to share in their suffering empathetically. The sorrow we feel with others and for others may then act as the fuel from which the flame of genuine compassion arises. If we never share in others' sorrow and pain, we have callously succumbed to indifference, but if we dwell in that suffering, we empathetically succumb to the near enemy of compassion, which does not help others, but only disempowers ourselves. To take others' suffering as my own means to respond to it as if it were my own; this means not with sadness, but with wisdom and compassion, which draws on my power to do what I can. Maybe the best I can do for the time being is to continue in meditation to bring out these qualities of wisdom, compassion, and power in my mind, so when the time comes to act I can be all the more effective. Maybe it's time to make a more active response. But there is no point at all in simply dwelling in sadness.

"What can I do?" is the question of human life. It's a perpetual question and there's obviously no single answer. For each situation that arises, if we apply whatever wisdom and understanding we have, with whatever loving-kindness and ability we can muster at that time, then we find the answer. The answer is whatever is the best we can come up with for the time being. It remains in flux because hopefully, if we are developing, then the answer will be different a year later. And always, the situation will be different.

Our culture seems to say that if you don't feel sadness at another person's distress, you must be indifferent or lacking in emotion. Sadness is falsely equated with compassion. If I were suffering from an illness, and a friend came to me in tears, saying how sorry she felt, it would not do me one bit of good. But if instead she offered me some remedy, I'd be very interested. The sadness by itself is just not useful.

The story of the birth of Tārā from a teardrop is a beautiful poetic expression of exactly this point. Avalokiteśvara was a great *bodhisattva*, who embodied awakened, limitless compassion, and who worked to alleviate the suffering of all beings. For lifetime after lifetime, over billions of years, not only on our planet, but in countless worlds, Avalokiteśvara applied himself, attending to each sentient being, striving to be of service. After eons had gone by, he paused to take stock and examine the fruits of his labors. When he looked around at the vast expanse of countless sentient beings, he saw the suffering was still endless. He burst into tears, and out of one of his teardrops arose Tārā, who embodies dynamic compassion in action. And she said to him, "Don't despair, I'll help you." When the spirit of Avalokiteśvara is articulated in words, it becomes the *mantra* OM MAṆI PADME HŪM.

When I consider how the Dalai Lama deals with the massive grief of his own country, I know there are rare occasions when, like Avalokiteśvara, he simply bursts into tears. I remember him talking about a group of fifteen or twenty recently arrived refugees who had an audience with him. They were telling their beloved teacher and leader of the cruelty and torture that they had experienced, and as they told the story, they burst into tears at the memory. The Dalai Lama described the scene, "They burst into tears, and then I burst into tears, and we all wept together." But as he told the story he was chuckling, and he looked almost euphoric. What had happened was an episode: it came, it passed. But what seems to be his steady ground state is a buoyant lightness in the face of the military occupation of his homeland, and the exploitation and torture of his people. That's his response. If instead he were to have succumbed to grief over the past thirty years, it would be justifiable, but I think he would then be useless, and Tibetan culture might not have survived in exile. His example gives me confidence that grief isn't necessary. It's not useful to ourselves or others. Instead, persevere with buoyancy, with lightness, and with strength.

QUESTIONS AND RESPONSES: CATHARSIS, LOGIC, AND COMPASSION

Question: The release of the emotion of sadness in weeping makes one feel so good after it's over; it can be an amazingly uplifting experience. You can release so much in such a short period of time and all of a sudden you have a whole new perspective. Are you saying that we can transcend that whole process altogether, that sadness is never necessary?

Response: Just as Śāntideva comments that sadness may act as the fuel for anger, it may also act as the fuel for compassion. I believe it is deeply human, in the best sense of the term, to share in others' sorrow, but I see no point in dwelling in sadness as a ground state of the mind that is aware of the suffering in the world. It is crucial to be aware of the extent and depth of suffering in the world, and the ignorance and the evil that are its sources, all of which are massive. That may seem an invitation to a ground state of sadness, but if we are actually to be of service and to live wholesome lives, and grow and bring forth our potential, I think the ground state needs to be more one of buoyancy, strength, and lightness.

In a roomful of weeping people, the Dalai Lama himself weeps. When he was recounting the story, there was no implication that he had done something wrong, or that his practice had failed in this. It simply happened. That spontaneous episode coming to flower was equally part of the practice.

The tears flow; it's clean and it's over, and the ground state is restored. That seems healthy. If weeping surges up in you, there is no point in trying to suppress it. One need not always remain in a ground state. But a ground state of buoyancy with occasional episodes of weeping is a healthier balance than a ground state of misery with occasional buoyancy.

Question: I've heard His Holiness the Dalai Lama say he believed the fundamental human nature is compassion. And I've heard him say also that our beginnings in this lifetime come from two people coming together in love. This has bothered me for a long time because marriages throughout centuries have been arranged, not because people love each other, but for reasons of power and patriarchal belief in possession. When you look as far back as we can look for this planet, and these civilizations, it seems that people coming together in love is the exception rather than the rule. And if that's the foundation, what does his argument stand on? Likewise he says we have communities because people care for each other. But communities have evolved more from the need for self-protection and survival, based on selfishness rather than compassion. It sounds like a faulty syllogism, but I think he has intuition that I'm not seeing.

Response: If one views the human condition from a mundane perspective, I agree with you that the evidence does not compel one to conclude that compassion is our fundamental emotion. Likewise, if we view human history from such a perspective, we may find no compelling reason to substantiate the metaphor that our existence is like a lotus with a jewel in it. There is too much contradictory evidence, and yet in the midst of human suffering and evil, the metaphor survives. The Tibetans have suffered their own genocide, and they are still using the same metaphor. I believe His Holiness was making this observation from the purity of his own vision, which is loftier and nobler than a mundane perspective. Such pure vision is consciously cultivated in the practice of Vajrayāna, and it draws on our own intuitive wisdom, our *buddha*-nature.

When we hear such a statement, that compassion is the fundamental human emotion, or that the essential nature of mind is pure, what affirms the statement in us is the very reality we are affirming. Our own innate compassion affirms its own reality. It is our *buddha*-nature affirming itself, and it does not rely on evidence. It percolates up, an inexorable force rising through all the millennia of contrary evidence, saying, "Nevertheless, I affirm, because I know it from the depths of my being." All the evidence to the contrary consists merely of adventitious obscurations of our innate purity.

Even the mental distortions of craving and of hostility can be seen as expressions of the *buddha*-nature gone awry. The source is good, but then when its expressions flow through our afflicted mind, they become warped and at times terribly harmful. Take the example of the Chinese genocide in Tibet. If we look deeply, at some level they were trying to do something good; they just had very warped ideas about how to do it. But they're not trying to do something bad. This may be why Jesus Christ said, "Father, forgive them, for they do not know what they are doing." People become deluded. Let us forgive them and ourselves for that and then tap in to what's beneath the delusion, and try to nurture that and bring it out.

COMPASSION FOR A SUFFERING PERSON: MEDITATION

The meditation for the cultivation of compassion is presented in a slightly different format than for loving-kindness. Whereas loving-kindness practice starts with yourself and then progresses to others, here you begin by bringing to mind a person you know who is suffering adversity, whether physically or mentally. Bring this person to mind as vividly as possible, and picture the whole situation. Attend to this person and let a yearning arise for this person to be free of suffering and the sources of suffering. Don't start the practice by focusing on a person you dislike, but simply someone who you know is suffering. Then apply this meditation to a dear friend, then a neutral person, and finally, towards a hostile person.

Throughout the practice of all of the Four Immeasurables, the theme continues: "As for myself, so for others. As I wish to be free of suffering, so do others wish to be free of suffering." Śāntideva comments, "I should eliminate the suffering of others because it is suffering, just like my own suffering. I should take care of others because they are sentient beings, just as I am a sentient being."[19] Whether a specific instance of suffering is my own or others' is not the central point, for in reality suffering has no private, individual owner. Śāntideva is challenging the notion that your suffering is irrelevant to me, that we are not connected. He continues: "If one thinks that the suffering that belongs to someone is to be warded off by that person himself, then why does the hand protect the foot when the pain of the foot does not belong to the hand?"[20] If your right hand itches, the left hand doesn't just lie there and say, "It's your problem. Scratch yourself."

Not only the human community is relevant here; Buddhists take into account all sentient beings, human and otherwise. So we are part of a community of sentient beings, like a body with organs and limbs and cells. The point is not to ignore our own well-being but to gain a bigger perspective on how our well-being fits into the greater community. Concern for our own well-being doesn't necessarily decrease, it simply fits into a bigger picture.

Even though Buddhaghosa recommends starting this practice by bringing to mind someone who you know is suffering, it may be helpful nevertheless to start with oneself. Look to yourself: Do you have any suffering you want to be free of? Any anxieties, any problems, any sources of distress, physical or mental? Are there any things that you fear? Do you wish you were free of these things? In all likelihood you will say: Yes, I'm very interested in being free of that. Having experienced this yearning to be free of suffering, we can recognize what we are talking about and then bring to mind another person who is suffering. Just as I wish for myself, so may you be free of suffering.

To make the meditation more complete, it is helpful to work with light. This is a prelude to Vajrayāna practice, in which visualized light is used a great deal. As you bring to mind a person suffering, and bring forth the desire that he or she be free of suffering, imagine your body saturated with light. Filling your own body with the light of your own *buddha*-nature, bring to mind the yearning: May you be free of suffering. Then imagine this light extending to the person suffering, and imagine that person being freed from the suffering and its source. Then, during the latter half of the session, send your mind out to the four quarters as before.

EXTENDING THE MEDITATION ON COMPASSION

Beyond attending to a suffering person, another access to the practice involves attending to someone who is engaged in very harmful action—action dominated by malice, self-centeredness, greed, jealousy, or cruelty. There may very well be some overlap between the person you choose here and the enemy chosen in the final stage of the cultivation of loving-kindness. In that case, these two practices become seamless, and one begins where the other one ends.

Bring vividly to mind a person who, as far as you can tell, really does engage in very harmful actions, whose mentality is afflicted with qualities such as malice, jealousy, spite, or selfishness. What is it that makes this person appear so vile? It could be his behavior, disposition, certain mental traits that we surmise dominate him. Don't turn from those qualities that are so abhorrent that they may provoke sadness, rage, or resentment. Then briefly bring your awareness back to yourself and imagine what it would be like if you yourself were afflicted with a similar disposition, similar habits of behavior. You may sense your horizons shutting down, your world growing smaller, your heart becoming contorted. You may sense the pain and anxiety that ensue from such affliction. Yearn to be free of these afflictions of the mind, unencumbered by such behavioral tendencies. Restore yourself to light and imagine being utterly free of them. Once again, sense the spaciousness, the lightness, the buoyancy, the soothing calm of freedom from those afflictions.

Turn your awareness back to the same person, and let the yearning arise, "Just as I wish to be free of such afflictions and harmful behavior, may you also be free." Look to the person who is afflicted, without equating the person with the temporary afflictions of personality and behavioral patterns. Look to the person, who, like yourself, simply yearns for happiness, and wishes to be free of suffering. Let your own desires fuse with those of this person: "May you indeed be free of suffering. May you find the rich happiness and well-being that you seek. May all the sources of unhappiness and conflict fall away. May you be free of suffering and its sources."

Like the sun appearing through a break in the clouds, like a blossom bursting forth from dark soil, imagine this person emerging from the suffering and from the sources of suffering that you find so repugnant. Imagine this person as vividly as you can, free of those sources of suffering. Now expand the scope of this compassion to all sentient beings in each of the four corners, attending first to the reality that each one essentially wishes to be free of suffering. It is this yearning that accounts for such diverse behavior, some of it wholesome, some of it terribly injurious. Let your heart be joined with their essential yearning. "May you indeed be free of suffering, just as I myself wish to be free of suffering." Let your body fill with light and send it out to each of the four quarters. Imagine sentient beings in each of these regions emerging from suffering and the source of suffering.

INTRUSIVENESS IN THE PRACTICE OF COMPASSION

The question of intrusiveness can be raised regarding this practice: What right do I have to impose my views and desires on another person's life? The question is valid, and the practice must encompass a respect for the other person's wishes. But in attending to a person who is suffering, we can ask ourselves whether this person wishes to suffer. Does this person delight in, or take nourishment from his or her suffering, whether caused by mental or physical afflictions? If the answer sincerely is no, then we can send out our wishes of compassion and kindness without reservation: May your own yearning to be free of suffering, and the sources of suffering, be fulfilled.

I take this very seriously. I don't want to be interfering in people's lives, neither as a teacher nor psychically, in imagination. It is inappropriate. But if I focus on other people's own wish to be free of suffering, then I feel there is no imposition as long as my own wish supports theirs. Objectively, what are the odds that my meditation is going to bring about some major shift in another person's life? Not great at all. But that's not the chief point of the practice. The purpose of the practice is to overcome any type of malice or cruelty in our own minds, and to transform our minds so that compassion or kindness arises without impediment. What are the chances of such a practice decreasing any inclination towards cruelty, and nurturing tendencies of kindness and compassion? The odds are very good.

MEDITATION ON AVALOKITEŚVARA, THE EMBODIMENT OF COMPASSION

In Buddhism, Avalokiteśvara is regarded as the embodiment of compassion. The Tibetans translate his name as Chenrezig (sPyan ras gzigs), meaning "one who watches with a steady gaze." A number of the Buddhist *sūtras* refer to Avalokiteśvara as a great *bodhisattva* on the path. In the *Heart Sūtra*, for example, the Buddha enters into a dialogue with Avalokiteśvara, and they discuss emptiness, or ultimate truth. Also very frequently in Tibetan Buddhism you hear of various lamas referred to as embodiments of Avalokiteśvara. Those are people who embody compassion and express it through their lives. Of course, the best known example is the Dalai Lama; millions of Tibetans simply consider him to be Avalokiteśvara.

Traditionally, at the beginning of any meditation, we set the motivation for the ensuing practice. In a meditation on compassion, this comes into full flower. Recognize the great need of sentient beings, the great degree of delusion, the sources of suffering in the world, and the perpetuation of suffering. Recognize this with the yearning: "May all sentient beings be free of this suffering and the sources of this suffering. May they be irrevocably free, not just temporarily, from their suffering and pain. In order to be most effective in relieving the suffering of others and bringing each one to a state of ultimate well-being, I aspire to attain enlightenment." Apply this noblest of all motivations to the practice. Be it ever so modest a practice, the motivation sets the direction and one begins to move towards that end.

To begin the practice itself, in the space in front of you, bring to mind Avalokiteśvara, as vividly as you can conceive him. In your mind's eye imagine this being of light, radiant with joy, gazing upon you with fathomless warmth and affection, delighting in your wholesome activities, filled with loving-kindness for each of us. Here is an embodiment and a window on the compassion that pervades all of reality.

As you chant the *mantra* OM MAṆI PADME HŪM, imagine a cascade of light coming forth from the heart of Avalokiteśvara, "the one who watches with a steady gaze." This cascade of light is of the nature of immutable joy, of compassion, and of purification. Imagine this light coming to the crown of your head, and then flowing down through your body, saturating every cell of your body and immediately dispelling any type of negativity, any impurity or trace of previous unwholesome actions that you have engaged in. It dispels any affliction of the mind, any imbalance of the body, and it saturates your body so that at the end of the chanting you sense your own body to be purely a body of this white light.

Now, at your invitation, imagine Avalokiteśvara diminishing in size to the height of about one inch, coming gradually to the crown of your head, and there instantaneously facing in the same direction as yourself. Imagine a soft, glowing white eight-petalled lotus at your heart, in the center of your chest, and invite Avalokiteśvara to dwell in the lotus of your heart. Imagine that he accepts gladly, dissolving into a shaft of light, coming down through the central channel to the *cakra* at your heart, and forming again there as Avalokiteśvara seated in the meditation posture on the lotus. Imagine a tiny pinpoint of radiant white light at the heart of Avalokiteśvara, the light of your own *buddha*-nature, the fount of all your innate wisdom and compassion and power. Like a supernova from a single point, imagine white light radiating in all directions, white light of the nature of joy, of compassion, and of purification. It radiates out, filling your body immediately to saturation point, and then extends out through every pore of your body, above and below and to all sides, reaching out to every sentient being around you.

Imagine that as soon as this light touches these sentient beings it suffuses them, removing their suffering and the sources of their suffering, and fulfilling the deepest desires of each one. Imagine this light suffusing every one around you, and then rapidly extending in all directions, out over the land surrounding you, touching every sentient being, every human, animal, and any other type of sentient being who may be present. It extends rapidly out in all directions over the globe, and then continues out beyond this world, out through our solar system, beyond the galaxy to all the infinite worlds, out to limitless space. Imagine the entire universe suffused with this light. Imagine the universe in the nature of light, and now dissolving into a shimmering light.

Imagine this universe now retracting, back into your body, so that only your body of light remains, with Avalokiteśvara at your heart. Let your own body dissolve into the body of Avalokiteśvara. Let the body of Avalokiteśvara dissolve into the seed of light at his heart, and let this seed of light dissolve into empty space of infinite energy. And now from this emptiness, imagine reforming your own body as a body of light, but now it is a softly glowing light, serene and yet invincible, unassailable. Within this body note the movements of energy associated with the breath. For the rest of the session, place the mind simply and quietly on these sensations of the rhythm of the breath.

Chapter Six
Empathetic Joy

REJOICING IN OTHERS' HAPPINESS

Striving in spiritual practice to cultivate meditative quiescence and cultivate such qualities as loving-kindness and compassion is certainly a worthy pursuit. Having ideals and goals may provide inspiration, direction, and coherence to one's life, but it can also lead to ambition and to frustration about not making progress fast enough. So it's good to balance such striving with an aspect of the practice that has nothing to do with goals and achievements, and one such practice is the cultivation of empathetic joy (*muditā*).

This is simply the act of rejoicing in the well-being of others. We do this frequently with loved ones, with our children and good friends. Watching a little puppy playing with a ball, its tail wagging back and forth, makes you smile. Even that is empathetic joy. It's not some strange Buddhist technique we have to learn totally anew. There is a closely related practice from the Indo-Tibetan tradition called rejoicing in virtue and its consequences. I'll discuss these first separately, and then see how they very easily can converge into one practice.

In the Theravāda tradition, the practice of empathetic joy is so straightforward that you would hardly think it's a practice. And yet, why not? You begin by bringing to mind a joyful acquaintance of yours—a person who is normally buoyant, lively, happy. It could be a friend; it could be a holy man or woman. The Dalai Lama is a very good example of someone who is radiantly buoyant almost all the time. Or the person you choose could be simply an acquaintance or a colleague. If you don't know any such people, I'll have to introduce you to some! Bring such a person vividly to mind and reflect on the quality of his or her life, the lightness and good cheer that this person brings to the environment and to other people. Then empathetically enter into that same joy, share it, rejoice in it, take delight in it.

You begin there and simply dwell on that joy in a relaxed way. This isn't a practice with stages to be accomplished; you just enjoy it! If you do wish to grow in this practice, after attending to a naturally joyful person, you move to a neutral person, and then finally direct your attention to a hostile person. You bring to mind occasions when this hostile person has been really happy, and if you can enter joyfully into this person's happiness—even if it's very rare—that brings a real transformation of mind. Obviously, even in a hostile person you look for a happiness that is wholesome or at least neutral. There are people who take delight in inflicting suffering on others; this is not a delight with which to empathize.

Eventually you extend the practice globally: wherever there is happiness, you delight in it. It's a very simple practice. Little needs to be said about it, but this doesn't mean it is not significant or valuable, especially in daily life. For example, I regularly watch the news to see how the world is getting on. There are possibilities for practicing all Four Immeasurables in that time slot, depending on what comes up. When I see someone really striving for happiness, the response is loving-kindness; when I see someone in despair or engaging in evil, then it's compassion. Happily, there are some news programs that try to end on something wholesome, and I make a point of rejoicing when they focus on some virtue. That's my time for empathetic joy. Whether it's reading newspapers, or hearing a story from a friend, hearing the latest shenanigans of our politicians and so on, you can always respond in one of those four ways, instead of cynicism, contempt, abhorrence, and despair—the other "four immeasurables."

The "near enemy" of any of the Four Immeasurables in Buddhism is a mental state that can arise by mistake as you are engaging in the practice. The near enemy may have some qualities in common with the quality you wish to cultivate, but in fact it's really quite different and will lead you in a different direction. The near enemy of empathetic joy is frivolity. It's not malignant, but it doesn't have the depth and the benefit of genuine empathetic joy. The "far enemy" consists of cynicism and despair combined. Just as cruelty is the opposite of compassion, and ill will is the opposite of loving-kindness, there is no possibility of cynicism and despair being present simultaneously with empathetic joy. They are mutually exclusive. In *The Path of Purification*, the distant enemy of empathetic joy is said to consist of aversion and boredom. I believe these are close kin to cynicism and despair.

REJOICING IN VIRTUE

The Tibetan Buddhist tradition also speaks of empathetic joy, but it places even more emphasis on rejoicing in virtue, which is the root of happiness. They say this is a direct antidote for jealousy, inasmuch as jealousy is the inability to bear another person's happiness and success. Note that in the Theravāda practice, the first step is focusing on a joyful person other than yourself. In the Tibetan Buddhist practice of rejoicing in the good, it's perfectly appropriate to start with yourself. This is a tremendously rich practice, and it's so simple. There's no notion of achievement, you just do it and it's immediately beneficial.

Rejoicing, especially when directed towards our own virtues, entails looking back on our own behavior, our aspirations and yearnings, then pausing and just delighting where we note that they are wholesome in nature. Maybe you've practiced meditation with a pure motivation and derived some benefit from it. Rather than just moving on, attend to your past practice, recognize that you have done something good, and take delight in it.

In attending to your virtuous aspirations, actions, and their results, you are not thinking, "I'm really a fantastic person; I'm probably better than most other people." That's a near enemy of rejoicing in virtue: self-adulation, arrogance, and conceit. It goes awry through a process of reductionism, in which you forget about all the causes and conditions that came together to make the virtue occur. Imagine if after a really good retreat, in which you gained a lot of insight, you came away from it thinking: "I'm really great! I bet nobody else did as well in meditation. In fact, I should be a teacher." When this happens, you are ignoring the context in which your experiences arose: the help of the teacher, the group support of the other meditators, and everything else. You have reified yourself, and then it's a problem.

True rejoicing in one's own virtues is profoundly different: it is always contextualized. If, for example, you have done a retreat, or gone out of your way to be of service, your attention includes the context, including the people who have helped and inspired you in your pursuit of excellence. Within that context you delight in the deed and the event. Then your joy is as clean as a whistle.

This very act of rejoicing itself acts as an inspiration to further your practice. You may look back after some months or years of meditation practice, and note: this used to be terribly difficult, and now it's not particularly difficult at all. You may find that the loving-kindness practice was ineffective when you first began, and now—lo and behold!—it emerges through your practice. Where we note there is some improvement, some transformation taking place, we can rejoice in that, acknowledge it, attend to it, make it part of our reality. This can provide grounds for some confidence, a sense of our own capacity that can also help to undermine jealousy. And of course this kind of rejoicing is also a direct antidote to self-denigration.

You don't stop there. Bear in mind that skill in meditation is only one aspect of spiritual practice. It is also worthwhile to rejoice in your own practice of ethical discipline. Looking back on your life, if you can recognize that you used to be very clever in sarcasm, abuse, and slander, but you don't do it any more, that's tremendous progress. It's a great achievement. Rejoice!

As you attend to your own practice, be it in ethics, in *samādhi*, in wisdom or compassion, you can also attend to others' practice in the same light. When you hear of someone else doing very well, pause and rejoice in that. This acts as a direct antidote for jealousy. This practice is excellent in an active way of life. There is so much, both in the media and in our personal experience, that easily arouses a response of sadness or grief, but whenever we see some virtue, attending to these bright spots draws them into our reality. Allowing ourselves to rejoice in it can be a real source of inspiration. Especially as an engaged practice, it is very, very useful.

You can begin this meditation with the approach taught in the Theravāda tradition, bringing to mind first a joyful person, and then attending to a neutral person, and then, if possible, to a hostile person. Don't move through this progression too quickly, or it may lead to hypocrisy.

Another avenue is just to pause and look at your life. Start there and ask if there is anything wholesome happening here, anything meaningful. If there is, attend to that and rejoice in it. Then, take yourself as an example and extend the thought to others: Like myself, so for you. Take delight in others' happiness, as well as in any effort they make to sow the seeds of their future happiness.

Chapter Seven
Equanimity

EQUANIMITY IN THERAVĀDA BUDDHISM

This final practice is translated as *equanimity* or *impartiality*, but each catches a different nuance of the original Sanskrit term *upekṣā*. In the very early years of my studies with Geshe Rabten in Dharamsala, he gave me just two topics to contemplate for months and months. One was a discursive meditation on the preciousness and rarity of a human life, with all its opportunities for practicing Dharma. The second was equanimity. This is not simply a feeling of indifference, devoid of pleasure or pain. Impartiality is perhaps the better translation, for it contrasts with the biased way we usually view other sentient beings. Loving-kindness, for example, is usually partial in day-to-day life. We commonly feel loving-kindness only for certain types of people: people who are nice to us, agreeable and friendly. When they smile at us, we smile back! We are indifferent to others less warm, and hostile to those whom we perceive as hostile. This division of all sentient beings into class one, two, or three, Geshe Rabten pointed out, is a major cause of our own distress.

Tibetan Buddhism speaks of the wisdom aspect of the practice, and its method aspect. Method, or skillful means, covers everything other than wisdom: compassion, generosity, faith, enthusiasm, service, and all other good qualities. Impartiality, or evenmindedness, is especially indispensable for the method aspect of one's spiritual practice. I'm speaking of it fairly briefly here, because in a sense we have been addressing it all along. The practice of loving-kindness was not limited to loving a friend, but rather loving yourself, a friend, a neutral person, and a hostile person. Compassion and empathetic joy were extended in the same way towards yourself, a loved one, a neutral person, and a hostile person. See if you can develop this even sense regarding everyone. It really is utterly indispensable if you want to open the heart completely. Equanimity rounds off the other three immeasurables—loving-kindness, compassion, and empathetic joy—and brings to them a profound state of balance.

The Path of Purification presents a technical discussion of equanimity as a specific contemplative achievement that is developed after you have attained the third meditative stabilization in loving-kindness. At this point, you start by attending to a neutral person toward whom you feel no particular attraction or repulsion. Then, you attend to a person you love and then to a hostile person, and see in each case if you can bring the same calm evenness of mind to bear, with no attraction or aversion.

If I stopped right there, one might say that it sounds rather impoverishing. We have just flattened our feelings for all our friends. Your mother walks in the door and you say: "Hello, what can I do for you, madam?" Isn't it better to have affection and attraction to people? It sounds like one giant step backwards for humankind. But it's not, and to see why, we need to go deeper.

Let's look at the near enemy of this equanimity, or impartiality. The near enemy is stupid indifference. We probably have experienced this at times, and we know people for whom it seems fairly characteristic. They watch the news, they see what's happening in the world, and they just don't care. When they see somebody else suffer injury, say in a traffic accident, they think: "I'm not going to touch him and get sued." They walk away and it doesn't faze them. Or they see something wonderful happen, and they don't care. That's stupid indifference, the near enemy. It may look superficially like the equanimity that is a very noble achievement of the mind, but it's only on the surface, and fundamentally it is utterly different. The far enemy of equanimity is attraction and revulsion, in which the heart reaches out towards some and rejects others. Equanimity, however, is like an utterly calm ocean: the mind is completely even.

EQUANIMITY IN TIBETAN BUDDHISM

In the Tibetan tradition, equanimity is not couched in an esoteric, highly advanced contemplative category, but rather is presented as the foundation of the Spirit of Awakening, or *bodhicitta*, which is at the core of all Mahāyāna spiritual practice. This is the central theme and motivation for the *bodhisattva* way of life, a whole mode of spiritual practice based on altruism and service.

All religious people would agree that altruism and compassion are extremely important, but there are different ways of regarding them. One way is to view them as a path of purification. Recognizing loving-kindness and compassion as effective antidotes to ill will and cruelty, we adopt them as vital components of our spiritual practice that will aid us in striving for insight, purification, and some degree of liberation. We attend first to our own problems, and as if we were ill, we take compassion and loving-kindness as medicine to restore the balance of our mind. Once we have achieved some greater health for ourselves, we then consider how we might be of service, and the service we can offer at that point may well be excellent.

Regarding love and compassion as a means to one's own purification has its own integrity that is not to be denigrated. The *bodhisattva* path, however, has a different flavor. Right from the very beginning it addresses the reality that our individual existence is already contextual, and that by our very nature we are related to others. Our own well-being is related to others' well-being. Our own identity, our own existence, is one of interdependence. From this vantage point, as soon as you open your eyes you see a tremendous amount of suffering in the world, while every sentient being yearns for happiness. One can't help but wonder how to be of greater service. Shall I go to medical school? Shall I learn how to be an excellent cook? There are many good ways to be effective in service and many things that need to be done. In the midst of all that— not as an alternative to it—there is a way to draw out your full capacity for service by developing the power of the mind. *Śamatha* is a key to drawing forth your own wisdom and compassion. Trying to be of service without wisdom is ineffective; trying to serve with intelligence but without compassion is dangerous.

To be of most effective service, we need to transform ourselves. Right now, our limitations are severe, and the needs of others are great; we need to reduce the limitations as far as possible. So, from the very beginning, we cultivate *bodhicitta*, attending to the needs of all other sentient beings, considering how to be of benefit and service. In order to be of greatest effectiveness, we may draw inwards to bring our wisdom and power to fulfillment; but altruism and service are central to the practice from the very beginning, and they give the practice its flavor.

Bodhicitta is the really key component. Kunu Lama Rinpoche, who gave His Holiness the Dalai Lama the oral transmission of *A Guide to the Bodhisattva Way of Life*, devoted his whole life to the development of *bodhicitta*, so much that he embodied that sublime spirit. Some people will devote their lives to a single practice, be it *śamatha* or some esoteric Vajrayāna practice, but this man made his whole practice the cultivation of *bodhicitta*. What this entails is cherishing the whole world more than you cherish yourself. You orient yourself entirely to turning your own being into a more and more effective tool for service. Kunu Lama Rinpoche wrote a short text in which he praises *bodhicitta* in a myriad of ways. If you wish happiness for yourself, he writes, or if you wish happiness for other people, develop *bodhicitta*. This is the key, this is the crown jewel of all spiritual practice. He was so deeply experienced in this practice that the Dalai Lama sought him out and received teachings from him. If the Dalai Lama comes to you for teachings on compassion, you've accomplished something.

The motivation of *bodhicitta* expresses itself very simply: May I attain the highest possible enlightenment for the benefit of all creatures. This impulse flows from great loving-kindness and compassion. There's a difference between what we've called "immeasurable" loving-kindness (*maitri-apramāṇa*) and compassion (*karuṇā-apramāṇa*), which are extraordinary in their own right, and "great" loving-kindness (*mahāmaitri*) and compassion (*mahākaruṇā*). These are technical terms that have very specific meanings, and the distinction is not trivial. Immeasurable compassion yearns from the heart: May each sentient being be free of suffering and free of the source of suffering. If it is truly immeasurable, it does not distinguish between friends and enemies. It's immeasurable in the sense that it has no bounds, reaching out to every sentient being with a heartfelt yearning.

Great compassion goes a step further. It recognizes that all sentient beings have a *buddha*-nature. Not only do they all want happiness and freedom from suffering, but they could possibly achieve it. Why couldn't all sentient being be free of suffering and the sources of suffering? The heart reaches out and expands and embraces them in immeasurable compassion: May you be free! But great compassion goes further and takes on itself the responsibility: I shall make you free!

Now that's a very profound and problematic resolution, but that's exactly what is taught. Great compassion and great loving-kindness are not merely a wish but an assumption of responsibility. How can that lead to anything but cosmic frustration? When *bodhicitta* is misunderstood it can turn into cosmic egotism. If I, Alan Wallace, took on the responsibility to free every sentient being from all suffering, wouldn't that be simply foolish? I could never do it in the few more years I have to live. But this resolution goes to the deeper level of our own *buddha*-nature, which is eternal. Śāntideva prays: "For as long as space endures and for as long as the world lasts, may I live dispelling the miseries of the world."[21] That is great compassion: Why couldn't all sentient beings be free of suffering and the sources of suffering? May they be free! I shall free them!

The *buddhas* will be active until every sentient being is free of suffering. That's the only job they have to do: to bring all sentient beings to a state of spiritual awakening. Will that ever happen? The Dalai Lama says he doesn't know, but he also says, in the meantime, keep on trying.

Great loving-kindness finds a similar expression to great compassion. "Why couldn't all sentient beings be endowed with happiness, and the sources of happiness? May they be so endowed! I shall bring them together with happiness and the sources of happiness!" If they are to lead to *bodhicitta*, compassion and loving-kindness must arise from a plane that does not exclude any sentient being whatsoever. It has to include the most vicious and the most benevolent of human beings as well as all other sentient beings, without exceptions. May Hitler and Pol Pot be free. Of course we should want them to be free. What would be better than if the villains of our civilization were freed from all of their intense delusions and hostility? What would be greater for all of humanity than if Hitler had somebody to help him out as a youth, and free him from his severe delusions?

Equanimity is absolutely indispensable. From that even plane arises the cherishing of others, of the whole world. From equanimity one may cultivate great loving-kindness and great compassion, and from these *bodhicitta* arises. When *bodhicitta* arises spontaneously and effortlessly, suffusing your entire lifestyle, then you are a *bodhisattva*. And it is said that when a person becomes a *bodhisattva*, the *devas* rejoice.

How do we do it? It's not so easy. In fact, it can be very difficult, because some people are friendly while others are vicious. It's easy to like some people and it's not very easy to like others. They don't smile back! So it has to go deeper. If we continue to judge people on the basis of appearances and behavior, the endeavor is hopeless. Instead we have to return to a very simple truth: every sentient being desires happiness and desires to be free of suffering. That's the bottom line. To make that deep, heartfelt affirmation of the *buddha*-nature of each sentient being is life-transforming.

Can we recognize that every sentient being wishes for happiness? All of us, including the most despicable of people, do the things we do because we're seeking happiness and want to be free of suffering. We do the things that we do, sometimes harmful, sometimes very good, but invariably because we want to find happiness. In this quest we may act obsessively, with great confusion and delusion: can we develop equanimity towards ourselves? Can we affirm that fundamentally, through thick and thin, through highs and lows, each of us is seeking happiness? We need to reach that level of understanding for every being, cut right through the surface and recognize a kindred soul at the core: "You are just like me. You want to have happiness and be free of suffering. How can I help?"

Of course, people are more lovable who attend to, and value, the cultivation of loving-kindness and compassion. The very first audience I had with His Holiness the Dalai Lama pertained very closely to this topic. I wanted to ask something important, so his time would not be wasted, and I thought about something that was bothering me. I was a very young student, about twenty-two, and I'd been living in Dharamsala for all of a few months. Hard as I was studying, of course I hardly knew anything at all. But to people who had been there for only a couple of weeks, I was an old-timer. There were very few Westerners around, and most Tibetans didn't speak English. So, new people would sometimes come to me with questions, and not infrequently I could answer. I began to have the sense that I was special, but I could see it, like a bizarre little weed sprouting in my garden. I knew I would be tending this garden for many years to come, and I worried about this weed. Should I attack it with some kind of herbicide, or should I give up farming all together? It was clearly not something I wanted to cultivate.

That was the question I posed to His Holiness. I told him I didn't want to develop arrogance. If this sense of superiority was growing even as I was just getting started, what would it be like in ten or twenty years? Growing in wisdom and compassion is something extraordinary. After all, many people are not applying their lives heart and soul to the cultivation of wisdom and compassion. In a sense you are becoming outstanding, exceptional, and unusual. But if you start thinking, "I'm outstanding, exceptional and unusual," you've just shot yourself in the foot. It was a dilemma. I could fail and not grow in wisdom and compassion, or I could succeed, and fail in a different way.

His Holiness gave two responses. He said first: "Imagine that you are really hungry, and somebody prepares for you a nice, healthy, well-rounded meal. When you've eaten it all up, do you feel arrogant? Do you feel superior and conceited?" I said no. "You've come a long distance from the United States," he continued, "You have come here because you are seeking Dharma. You've come here spiritually hungry, looking for spiritual nourishment, and you're getting a full meal. But as you eat it, there is no reason to feel special or superior. Just feel happy!"

His second response pertains particularly to the issue of evenmindedness, equanimity, and impartiality. He said: "I am Tenzin Gyatso, and I am a monk. As a monk I have had special opportunities and excellent teachers. I've learned a lot of Dharma, and had many opportunities to practice, many conducive situations. And with that, I have an unusual responsibility. Now, here's a fly," and he pointed to a fly in the room. "Imagine another fly was eating a little drop of honey, and this fly came along and pushed him away, showing aggression, competitiveness, and total self-centeredness. What do you expect? (How many altruistic flies have you seen?) A fly has very limited opportunities. It's had no opportunities for learning any other kind of behavior, so you accept it. But if I should act like that fly, this is very inappropriate. Because I have had greater opportunities for understanding, for wisdom, for practice, for distinguishing wholesome from unwholesome, then I am obliged to act very differently from that fly!"

In this same context, a couple of years ago, His Holiness was asked by a reporter whether he has any peers. His answer was: "Yes. Everybody!"

This is equanimity. As we attend to people who show great resentment, hostility, or selfishness, we can pause and recognize that they have a *buddha*-nature like we do. They yearn for happiness, wishing to be free of suffering, like we do. Different causes and conditions have come together to make them act as they do—a different environment, a different personal history. But all this is in flux. Had I lived under those same conditions, lifetime to lifetime, that would be me. The result is a gentle evenness that sets into the mind.

In the Tibetan tradition, the actual technique for developing equanimity is not esoteric and highly technical, as Buddhaghosa explains. In the Tibetan Buddhist training, this evenness is the first step in the cultivation of the Spirit of Awakening, just as a farmer first levels the field so that all the water doesn't gather on one side and leave the other side dry. The first priority is an even field, an utterly fundamental and indispensable component of the practice. One technique they suggest is simply taking into account: "What are the causes and conditions that gave rise to this?" We return to that simple thing: "Each one yearns for happiness and to be free of suffering, just like myself."

There is another avenue to this that uses a traditional psychological approach. It entails bringing three people to mind, just as we've done in earlier practices: a loved one, a neutral one, a hostile one. First bring to mind a person you love, someone who can do no wrong in your sight. If you even see him do wrong you assume he must have had a bad day. As he walks through the door, a big smile comes to your face. You delight in him: thinking about him gives you happiness. And so you reflect upon this person. Naturally you are bound to have some attachment here, and it expresses itself as the hope that this person doesn't go away. Let that attachment arise, and then pause and question what here is so attractive. Why focus on this person when there are so many other fine people around? The particulars of this or that behavior will come to mind, but then pause again and recognize that perhaps twenty years ago this person was a stranger you didn't know at all. Another twenty years from now he may be just a memory for you. There's nothing special here to cling to. Certain causes and conditions came together, all of them in flux, and so this temporary episode occurs right now. I must emphasize that this is not designed to decrease or subdue any element of affection. Only the craving needs to be leveled, the special attraction that makes this person seem more worthy than everybody else.

Then shift to a neutral person. The person behind the cash register at your local market is a good example. Bring this person to mind and then ask yourself why you feel so neutral. Is it that this person's desires don't count? Does this individual have no personality? Is she not as real as your loved ones? We sense that we have very little relationship with this person. She has not done anything endearing to you, nor anything to make you feel hostile. But two years from now she could be one of your best friends, or a sworn enemy, if the causes and conditions come together. And so you recognize that it's just causes and conditions that place anyone, temporarily, in this neutral category.

Finally, the third case is one of the few instances in Buddhist practice in which you focus on a hostile person and arouse your own anger. You don't verbally express it or physically act on it, or in any way engage with this person; it's purely a thought-experiment. You bring the person to mind vividly, and admit that you think he's disgusting. Fill in all the reasons for your aversion, and let it emerge quietly. Then ask yourself, what's the basis for this? On this occasion, under these circumstances, these causes and conditions came together. Twenty years ago this person wasn't an enemy, but just another person. Twenty years from now, this person may be just a memory to you. Why should your mind be convoluted with suffering? It's just causes and conditions that come together and will pass in turn.

See if your mind can then be subdued, and return, not to a point of stupid indifference, but to one attending to a primary truth of our whole existence: each person, friendly, neutral, or hostile, wishes only to be happy and free of suffering, just as we ourselves do. We are equal, and we each deserve to be happy. If loving-kindness and compassion can arise on that basis, they arise like water spreading out on an even plane in all directions.

Note that the hostility you feel tends to arise first in response to a particular deed, a particular pattern of behavior. But then you extend it, and attach the actions to the person. "This person is so insensitive, so abusive!" we say until we believe: This a lousy person. Even if he were held in an isolation tank, he would still be a lousy person.

Behavior is temporary; it arises in dependence upon causes and conditions. If we believe that a person really is essentially rotten, based on our observation of his behavior, then we have equated a person with his afflictions. Causes and conditions can alter people's qualities, but we freeze them in time. We lock them in and equate them with certain negative characteristics. Then our hostility feels justified. It's as if the person would no longer exist if the behavior did not exist. To equate a person with behavior is unrealistic, and very harmful to ourselves. The point of the practice is never to equate any person with a form of behavior.

Let's go even closer to the bone: when someone is not doing anything, but we still feel he's disgusting. We have now equated a person not only with his behavior, but with his disposition. You may easily dislike, and feel justified in disliking, someone who is terribly brutal and abusive. Bring such a person to mind right now. This person is a terrible person because he harms other people. But what makes him brutalize others? It is this person's afflictions of hostility and delusion. So now we can ask: If this person wields a stick, and goes around beating people with it, do you get angry at the stick? Of course not; the stick had no choice in the matter. Śāntideva then counters: "Disregarding the principal cause, such as a stick and the like, if I become angry with the one who impels it, then it is better if I hate hatred, because that person is also impelled by hatred."

The crucial issue is to separate not only the behavior, but even the disposition and mental states, from the person. Recognize: here is a person who is afflicted. Then you can ask yourself who this person is, and apply wisdom in the analysis. Do people change? Were you the same when you were five years old, or ten, fifteen, twenty? You do change, and yet it's still meaningful to say that was you. You share a personal history with that five-year-old child.

Recognizing that a person grows and changes, we yearn for him to continue to change and eventually to be free of these afflictions, free of the behavior that these afflictions cause. That's an appropriate and meaningful response. If you want to penetrate further into what is called "ultimate analysis," you then ask: Who is this person? If the person is not the hostility, not the stick, then who is he? Upon investigation, you find no one who stands up under that kind of analysis. There's no core or real substance in there. That becomes potent in various ways, but especially as an answer to a strong sense of hostility towards another person. In hostility we tend to reify people, equating them with their negative qualities or behavior such that, temporarily, our own minds become deluded. Our horizons become very limited when it is impossible to imagine that a person could be freed from those characteristics. We have fused the person with the characteristics, creating an unrealistic cartoon character. If we were free of delusion, then hostility and aggression wouldn't have a chance to arise, because they grow out of delusion.

QUESTIONS AND RESPONSES: ON DISTINGUISHING ATTACHMENT FROM AFFECTION

Question: When you address yourself to the hostile person and try to take that feeling apart, such meditation will likely be conducive to loving-kindness and compassion. On the other hand, when you try not to be too attached to people whom you do like, how do you do that without introducing some unnecessary negativity?

Response: It's a good point. There is a subtle and crucial distinction between attachment and loving-kindness or affection. In the process of developing *bodhicitta*, one cultivates what is called "affectionate loving-kindness." When you feel affectionate loving-kindness for someone, when he walks into your presence, your heart opens, you're delighted, like a mother who sees her only child after a long period of separation. That's the quality of loving-kindness that a *bodhisattva* brings to every sentient being.

Experiencing such affection from another person may transform your life, and developing this quality is a crucial aspect of spiritual growth. Affectionate loving-kindness is filled with the awareness that each other sentient being is like yourself, a subject who wishes to be loved and to be happy. With that empathy, that feeling of kinship, you recognize each sentient being as a subject, not simply an object. Attachment doesn't deal with subjects, but rather with very attractive objects. It's very nice to look at a person and see them smile back. That's pleasant. Like looking at a beautiful bird or a flower, it makes us feel good. That's not to be confused with loving-kindness.

Attachment is concerned with objects. It's very nice to have people praise us. That praise is an object. It's very nice to have people smile at us. It's very nice to experience these pleasant stimuli, and when we do so, a sense of possessiveness easily arises. Like so many modern love songs say, "I love you so much, never leave me!" They don't say, "But if it's better for you to go off to college, you'd better go." What it's really saying is, "Don't leave me, baby, because you are very attractive to me. Looking at you, I get pleasurable sensations." This doesn't have much at all to do with loving-kindness, but it has everything to do with attachment.

There's an important distinction there, but it's not always easily discernable. By and large, our feelings for others are mixed, especially when it comes to our friends and loved ones. But we need to make the distinction and it requires the skill of a surgeon. You don't want to tamper with the affection, but you'd do well to lose the attachment.

Suppose a person for whom you have great affection turns resentful toward you for some terrible thing that has happened in his life, or perhaps just grows distant. You used to think he was wonderful, but now you're not so sure. The disappointment you feel stems from attachment. The purpose of this practice is to remove that element of attachment, like a skilled surgeon, while retaining and even enhancing affection. But they are very close together and it's difficult not to throw out the baby with the bathwater. Monks sometimes do that. A standard meditation to overcome lust focuses on the foulness of the body. That means, if you're a heterosexual male, you meditate on the female body as an assembly of bones, tissue, skin, blood, liver, spleen, urine, feces... yecch! The whole idea is to make it seem repugnant, so a woman's body looks to you like something hanging in a butcher's shop!

Equanimity is not easy. The whole point of equanimity is to sift out attachment on one side, and the repulsion on the other, leaving an even base so that genuine, selfless affection can grow.

Chapter Eight

The Empowerment of Insight

It is possible for the mind to become disempowered. It feels then as if reality is just a given, and all we can do is try to deal with it. Events seem simply to present themselves to a disempowered mind. It can recognize an event as an atrocity or as something wonderful, but all it can do is to like it or lump it. There is no sense of participation.

Scientific materialism encourages such a sense of disempowerment. The mind is acknowledged as no more than an epiphenomenon of the brain, having no potency of its own. Wherever the brain leads, the mind follows. Some external physical stimuli comes in, and the mind is just a recipient. This understanding of the mind is widespread in our society, especially in the media. Do you want to know why you suffer? It's in your DNA, it's in your brain, it's in your metabolism, it's something physical, we are told. Even our memories, hopes, and fears are lodged in the gray stuff of our brain. A disempowered mind just follows the flow of stimuli but has no active role of its own.

This ubiquitous view is implicitly an utter disempowerment of the mind, and of the whole notion of a participatory universe. Buddhism has never accepted this, nor have many other contemplative traditions. So I have a great deal of confidence that it is possible to turn the tables around: to begin empowering the mind with wisdom, and to recognize that the ways in which we attend to reality will shift the reality that we experience. As William James said, what we attend to becomes our reality. And we certainly have a choice about what we attend to when the mind starts to become empowered.

The disempowered mind feels it has no choice about what it attends to. It's compulsive. I once witnessed a tragic case, when I was invited by David Spiegel, a psychiatrist at Stanford, to observe a group session of women who had breast cancer. Probably all of them were going to die of breast cancer, but one of the women expressed it so poignantly. She had recently encountered a *Time Magazine* article that presented some apparently intractable statistics: If you have metastatic breast cancer, your chances of survival are marginal. This woman was now in that stage of cancer, and seeing this, her world was shattering before her eyes. She had thought she might have a chance, until she saw that article. And she felt devastated, completely disempowered. She said she wished she had never seen the article; it made her feel like she was helplessly lost. "My mind is torturing me with these statistics," she wept, "I wish I had some peace of mind, I wish I could control my mind. I wish I knew how to meditate." Upon witnessing this heartfelt plea, I wished that she had begun meditating earlier.

Training the attention is definitely one way to begin empowering the mind. There is an enormous power in being able to control the attention. Then, as we gain power over our attention, we come to know from our experience, not just as a belief, that we have power over the reality we attend to. And our reality starts to shift. As Śāntideva declares, by subduing one's own mind, all dangers and fears are subdued. That is something definitely within our reach, not just for advanced contemplatives in Tibet. In fact, empowering the mind is almost a misnomer. It's not as if you are doing something special to the mind to make it big and powerful. You are simply removing impediments, so the inherent power of the mind can spring forth. That is all that *śamatha* does.

There are, of course, further reaches of the mind's empowerment in *samādhi*. When those impediments are removed in very deep *samādhi*, then not only does what you attend to become your reality, but generations of Buddhist contemplatives have said that the mind has the potential to alter physical reality by the power of its attention. The tables are radically turned.

One wonderful way that power manifests is through healing. There are a myriad of other possibilities discussed in *The Path of Purification*.[22] These are not easy accomplishments, but nothing could persuade me that such potentials of the mind do not exist. It's high time in our civilization to recognize the profound role of participation and attention in the reality we experience.

When the power of the stabilized mind is united with the wisdom that comes from understanding the conceptually designated nature of reality, the result is extraordinary. Geshe Rabten, one of my foremost teachers, told me of one of his retreats many years ago. He was meditating on emptiness and gained some realization of this lack of inherent existence of phenomena. In other words, if phenomena were inherently existent, they would be absolutely objective and unrelated to the mind. But the Buddhist teachings on emptiness free us from this compulsion, recognizing there are no intrinsic realities in this world, no autonomous substances. That realization, to phrase it differently, points to the participatory nature of reality. Geshe Rabten was gaining access to an insight that there is nothing in and of itself that is independent of any kind of conceptual designation, nothing that is devoid of participation. Once you begin to realize that, it suggests an extraordinary, perhaps even limitless malleability in the nature of reality. Implicitly the mind becomes enormously empowered. This is the power of insight, different from the power of *samādhi*.

Another access to empowerment of the mind is faith. This is strongly emphasized in Judaism, Christianity, and Islam. Faith opens doors, just as samādhi and insight do. It's time that we started opening all of them, because our society has largely succumbed to the disempowerment of the mind.

Candrakīrti, an Indian Buddhist sage who lived perhaps in the seventh century, was a great master of the teachings on emptiness, one of the greatest in all Buddhist history. There is a story that once when he was giving teachings on emptiness and the role of conceptual designation, a student had some reservations about it. So Candrakīrti took out a piece of charcoal and drew a picture of a cow on the wall of his hut. And then he milked it!

Is it possible that physical reality can be so manipulated that one might actually do damage with one's mind by directing enmity towards another person? The Buddhist tradition says yes, and through the power of prayer one can also help others, even at a great distance, as claimed in Christianity, in which whole congregations may direct their prayers to others in great distress. That practice is encouraged in Western religions, and they are not doing it just to make their own minds better. The intention is that the prayer may be effective. I think it can be.

I emphasize the positive theme of helping others with one's mind, because that's something actually worth practicing. When a group of people do this together in concert—perhaps none of them have much *samādhi*—the effect is like many people shining many flashlights onto one spot, all from different angles. That spot gets warmer. That's one way to do it. Another way is to ask one person who has very deep *samādhi* to pray; that's like directing a laser. The Tibetans often do this, and it was also done traditionally in Judaism and Christianity.

If one person shines a light, it may be very difficult to see any effect. But don't count it out. You may really be surprised by what could happen. Not that you should accept as dogma that prayer works. Dogma is boring. But it would be really interesting just to try this and see what happens.

You can probably surmise that the converse is also true: one person's malicious thought could possibly do some damage, as could a whole group of people actively directing their enmity towards an individual or a community. I hope that no research is done on that. Let the research be done on the positive side, and let us avoid the negative like the plague.

The Buddha himself spoke of this negative power. He said that if a person who has attained the first meditative stabilization directs a thought of enmity, with that focused attention, towards another person, it can be lethal. The first stabilization is a very deep state of *samādhi* that is one step beyond *śamatha*. That's why, if you're cultivating *śamatha*, you should also do a lot of other practices such as the Four Immeasurables.

Of course, you would not be able to sustain *śamatha* while nurturing enmity. The power of the mind would soon start to dissolve. It's said that Devadatta, a relative of the Buddha who was once his disciple, had attained meditative stabilization before he developed strong jealousy for the Buddha. Once he developed this enmity, he lost his *samādhi*. You can't sustain enmity in pure *śamatha* practice, which is why it is such a good path. There seem to be forms of black magic, dating back well before Buddhism, that allow one to sustain enmity while empowering the mind. But as far as I know, you can't do this by means of the cultivation of *śamatha*.

I know very little about these techniques, and I'm not really interested. Generally speaking, in a traditional cultures such as you find in India, Nepal, Malaysia, Indonesia, and the Philippines, where there are pockets of an untouched ancient culture, you may find people who are still practicing these methods. I heard of such people when I was living in India, and I avoided them.

If you ever feel threatened by some malevolent force, which can happen in deep meditation, then bring to mind the most glorious spiritual being you know of, someone who radiantly embodies virtue, compassion, loving-kindness, and wisdom. Call on that being and say: "Now I'm relying on you!" The refuge is there.

Another problem can arise, especially as you go deep into *śamatha* practice. Like sending a probe down into a swamp, as you go through different strata of your mind you may hit a layer of sheer dread where everything that could possibly be a source of danger in your life rises up with a malevolence that seems completely inevitable. You feel you are about to be crushed, and if one thing doesn't demolish you, then another one will. It's easy to laugh at this now, but when it arises it's no joke. It is psychically dark and heavy. The Tibetan contemplative Gen Lamrimpa's advice on this is very clear: Don't identify with this fear; don't believe in it. This is a time for courage and strength. When you feel like a city besieged, under the battering ram of consuming despair and hopelessness, fill your body with light. Point at the darkness and say: You have no basis in reality. This takes courage.

When we began the one-year retreat, Gen Lamrimpa told the meditators: You may be visited during this year by demons, especially if you're progressing well in the practice. There are many traditional accounts of this; it's part of the territory. You learn how to deal with them, how not to succumb. The very engagement with them is part of the practice. In a sense, you need them. The Tibetans take this very seriously. If a yogi were to begin a retreat the first thing that person would do is perform a ritual offering on behalf of all the beings living in that area.

The notion of demons and such entities is not part of our contemporary Western world view, but dread, anxiety, abject fear, and hopelessness are. And when they appear, you need to respond in just the same way as if a grimacing demon was coming at you. The response is the same because that's what it is. The demons know how to appear to us so we take them seriously. Loving-kindness practice is also one of the greatest protections.

Sometimes you may have an irascible neighbor: one of the entities may not welcome you, and then you have to deal with it. That's what happened to Lobsang Tenzin, one of the very finest contemplatives I've ever known. His spiritual biography was extraordinary. He had joined the Indian military because he wanted to kill Chinese, but when he dropped that agenda there was nothing left for him to do besides attain enlightenment. He was utterly riveted on that goal, and all the rest of his life he worked at nothing else. With one hundred dollars saved from his military pay he bought himself some grain and lentils and went up to meditate in a damp cave above Dharamsala. A hundred dollars doesn't last all that long, even in India. When it was gone, the other yogis started taking care of him. They were all poor, but he was the poorest. And the word got around that he was very earnest, and that he was doing very well. He was up there for twelve years, gradually moving farther and farther back into the mountains. Eventually he lived in a cave a five-hour hike above Dharamsala. He would come down once a year to hear His Holiness teach, and to buy another bag of grain and lentils. Lobsang Tenzin had plenty of experience with demons, and he knew how to deal with them.

One way to deal with them is with enlightened ferocity. As Geshe Ngawang Dargye once said, "If you think that wrathful deities look frightening in a Tibetan *thangka* painting, you should see them in person!" Ferocity is a last resort, and it's different from simply getting angry or being malevolent oneself. Enlightened ferocity arises from bliss, and it is an expression of compassion, not a contorted expression of despair, rage, or frustration with the world. On the contrary, it's a mind that is completely undistorted. Recognizing that this is what's needed now, it expresses itself very powerfully. It's far more powerful than contorted anger.

FROM INSIGHT TO AN UNMEDIATED EXPERIENCE OF THE ULTIMATE

What is meant by self-existence? What are the criteria for determining what is and what is not self-existent, and how is this useful in practice? Phenomena may be either self-existent or they may exist as dependently related events. Let's see how these two interface. The term "dependently related event" has a very specific meaning in Madhyamaka, or "Middle Way," philosophy. If a phenomenon is a dependently related event— be it a human being, a galaxy, a mind state, or anything else— there are three ways in which it is said to exist as such.

First, something is a dependently related event in the sense that it arises in dependence on prior causes and conditions. For example, Alan Wallace is a sequence of dependently related events because, had my parents not existed, I wouldn't be here. They were here first and I am a product of their union. That's all it means: A precedes B, and if A had not existed, B could not have existed. If something were self-existent, then it would not require any preceding causes or conditions. That's simply how the term "self-existent" is understood in this context.

The second aspect of being a dependently related event concerns the relationship between the parts and the whole, or between the qualities of a phenomenon and that which bears the qualities. Any phenomenon that we can posit as existent has components. If it's a physical phenomenon with a definite location in space, for example, it has a front side and a back side. It has spatial dimensions and other characteristics. Even something that really doesn't have spatial dimensions, like a feeling of loving-kindness, can be described in terms of its attributes. Any phenomenon we can identify has components or qualities. If not, then how could we ever identify it? Please tell me how many schmorffles there are in front of you right now. Haven't a clue? Maybe there are trillions of them crawling all over the place, but you don't know; because first I have to tell you what a schmorffle is like. Once I identify its attributes, then you can start looking and say: "There's one!"

We identify phenomena by means of their attributes or components, and it is perfectly legitimate to say they *have* those components. An atom has a nucleus; it has a certain number of electrons; it has a charge. This is an appropriate and valid way to speak. An atom is a dependently related event because it is related to and dependent upon its own components. If you take away its electrons, its nucleus, its charge, and other attributes, there is nothing left over. Likewise, I am dependent upon my mind and my body. If you destroy this body, there is a continuum of consciousness that carries on, but it's no longer Alan Wallace. Alan Wallace died, and what remains is a continuum that shares some history with Alan Wallace's history. So that's a second facet of dependent origination. If something is self-existent, then it is sufficient unto itself, and not dependent on any components or attributes. It simply is, in and of itself.

The third aspect of dependent origination concerns the role of conceptual designation. In the process of identifying something, a conceptual and/or verbal designation takes place. We designate something as an atom, or as a feeling of loving-kindness, or whatever. Nothing is happening ontologically in this process: my identifying Christina does not bring her into existence in reality. But experientially, phenomenologically, by identifying Christina I draw her out from her environment. Visually, for example, I isolate patterns of color from the background and now Christina is visible, separate from the floor, separate from her clothes, recognizable as a person I have known for some years.

Identifying the existence of any phenomenon must involve conceptual designation. By saying that something exists, we draw it out from that which is not it. The phenomena themselves are not self-defining; they do not demand that we designate them in one and only one unique fashion. If they did, they would be self-defining, and the role of the conceptually designating mind would in that case be utterly passive. In fact, the role of consciousness, of our intelligence, our memory, our recognition, is by nature participatory. I could identify any phenomenon in a variety of different ways; by choosing one way I have effectively drawn boundaries around a certain set of attributes. If something were self-existent, it would draw its own boundaries; and if you were sharp enough, you would recognize where they are. That would be a purely objective discovery. But if something is a dependently related event, then the boundaries are malleable and it is the process of conceptual designation that imputes those boundaries, defining a phenomenon as bearing certain components and attributes.

Let's consider a certain phenomenon, for example Elise. Let's attend to Elise, as opposed to other things that are near Elise, or things that Elise has. For example, she has a car. That's not Elise. She has a sweater, but that's not Elise. She has hair, but that's not Elise. She has a head, but that's not Elise. But Elise is there. We can say we have demarcated Elise with that conceptual designation; we have brought Elise as a phenomenon into the field of our experience. But what's there apart from that conceptual designation of Elise? There's a body, but that is not the same as Elise. The body is another conceptual designation. It too has parts. What remains when we remove the grid of this conceptual designation, a "body"? It too has its own component parts. Remove that conceptual grid. There are cells. Remove that grid. There are atoms. Remove that grid. There are electrons. Remove that grid....

There was an assumption prevalent until about the turn of this century that if you were to remove all the grids you would be left with little tiny bits of matter. They would be self-defining: the basic building blocks of the universe that exist purely objectively. Everything else may be convention, just configurations of these basic building blocks, but really there is a hard core reality out there. But in this century physics came to the great revelation that when you look for the little building blocks, they don't exist independently of the system of measurement by which they are detected. Instead, what you see depends on the kind of conceptual construct you bring to the inquiry; if you shift your mode of inquiry, what you see is quite different. Moreover, the conceptual constructs—for example, light as a wave versus light as a particle—are not even compatible. One independent thing cannot be both a wave and a particle, for the properties of those two types of phenomena are radically different. Rather, in the context of one system of measurement, something may appear as a wave, and in another context it may display characteristics of a particle. But when we try to identify that "it" independently of any system of measurement, we come up empty-handed.

If something were self-existent, it would stand up under your most penetrating analysis. Because it is self-defining, you would be compelled to define it just as it defines itself. But dependently related events do not exist in that way. For us to posit: "That exists," the very statement is itself dependent upon the conceptual designation. So it already suggests a participatory nature.

At a deeper, more fundamental level we can challenge the very notion of existence versus nonexistence, which seems at first glance to fly in the face of common sense. For example, it wasn't too long ago that the planet Pluto was discovered. Common sense insists it was there all along; we just didn't know about it. Finally we got the right apparatus and discovered what was already there, in and of itself, way out on the periphery of the solar system. There's really such a strong sense that it was there, it was self-existent, and we just came along discovered it.

But what do we mean by "exists"? Even the very notion of existing is not self-defining. Two people in the last few days have shared with me extraordinary experiences they have had and both prefaced their account by saying, "Maybe it was my projection; maybe it wasn't real." What do we mean when we say something exists, and something else is just a projection? The events these people described took place. They weren't lying to me, or creating something out of nothing; they were narrating extraordinary experiences as closely as they could. The events took place, but do the phenomena they observed exist?

The notion of existence is one more conceptual designation. It's not self-defining. Whenever we can point to a phenomenon and say: "That exists," we've already brought our conceptual framework into play, because people do in fact have different notions of what "exist" means. When we say: "It exists," the meaning depends on the kind of conceptual framework in which it is asserted. It's not something simply presented to us by reality. Thus, "It exists" is a relational statement, not an absolute statement. Whatever it is, it exists only as a dependently related event.

Is this true of everything that we can bring to mind—including mind, God, Buddha, Dharmakāya, the cosmos, time, space, energy? Is there nothing at all that is self-existent? Does anything self-exist, autonomously, just waiting to be passively discovered by an observer? The Madhyamaka answer is no. Does this mean everything in the whole universe is just relational, simply a matter of convention? Is there no absolute? Is there nothing that transcends language? Is there nothing that transcends concepts? If we answer yes, then we have just used language to claim the existence of something that transcends language, which means it didn't transcend it at all.

There is a point at which thought and language must fall silent. This is not a denial of the effable, it's simply a refusal to play the game of trying to pin down the ineffable with language.

This becomes very interesting experientially, and is most easily accessible if you can stabilize this chatterbox mind with *śamatha* practice. If you can develop some degree of meditative quiescence, then you can start probing into the nature of identity, the nature of external phenomena, or even into the nature of awareness itself. As you probe, see if you can release even the concepts of "existent" and "nonexistent." Release even those as simply more conceptual constructions. See if you can delve into pure experience, leaving all conceptual frameworks behind.

We are playing with language here, because we are talking about an experience that has left talking behind, but we can ask: Does any experience exist that leaves behind all conceptual frameworks, all ideas, all concepts, all language, all demarcations, all this's and that's? Is there such a thing as unmediated experience? The Buddhist answer is yes, without question. But what does this mean? What would unmediated experience be like?

Let's consider the first-person accounts of such experience. All accounts will, of necessity, be inadequate. Experience that transcends language and conceptual frameworks can't be adequately described in the language it transcends. But can you say anything at all that is meaningful? Yes; such experience takes place. That is a legitimate statement. Can you describe what takes place? No, but you can say what doesn't occur: the sense of a duality between subject and object. The distinction between I, the meditator, attending to that separate object is dissolved. You can say that the experience entails bliss, the like of which you have never experienced before. But "bliss" is about as far as you can go with language before resorting to metaphor: "It is like empty space. It is like radiant light. It is unborn. It is spontaneous." All of those are only metaphors, but that's the best you can do.

How can one know whether it is possible through practice to transcend the sense of duality, to transcend language, to transcend experience mediated by concepts? The only way to know is to do it, and that is the challenge. The Buddha declared it is possible. You are not locked into your own personal history, your own conceptual and cultural framework. You have your own personal history but it's not the whole story. There is also a transcendent element to your being that can be accessed experientially, and it goes beyond all concepts. The experience is frequently described as pure awareness, but it's not awareness as part of a duality, such as mind and matter. It does not fit into the Cartesian game plan. If you access that experience by delving into the nature of awareness, then, coming out of it, you might describe it as unborn, spontaneous, nondual, uncontrived, unfabricated awareness. Moreover, when people come out of this experience, they tend to speak of the entire world, with all of its myriad diversity, arising from this primordial awareness. Such nonduality is the ground of being.

This approach, going right into the nature of the mind itself, is the path of wisdom. In Vajrayāna Buddhism there is also a path of energy, in which one realizes the very subtle primordial energy of one's being. As you realize that, you come to see the nonduality between that energy and primordial awareness. Eventually you reach the realization that energy and mind ultimately are nondual, and all of the universe, with all of its myriad diversity, its complexity, all of its many parts of galaxies and so forth, arises from this very subtle "energy/mind." From one vantage point it manifests as awareness, from another vantage point it arises as energy, but in fact they are nondual.

If one gains the depth of insight necessary for an unmediated experience of the ultimate, its impact upon one's own being and mind is radical. It's not simply a passing event that turns into a memory. It is radically and irreversibly transformative.

By that insight alone, which invariably is backed with a high degree of stability and vividness of mind, on returning to the phenomenal reality of "this and thatness," the mind continues to hold an enormous power of transformation over the physical world, because one knows from one's own experience the essential malleability of the physical world. It's possible to transform physical reality out of the sheer power of that realization. There are easier ways of transforming physical reality, without the full power of this insight. It can be done just with *śamatha*, which does not necessarily entail that depth of insight.

Śamatha is a modification of a natural phenomenon: consciousness. Like light or energy, consciousness is a basic ingredient of reality. In *śamatha*, you purify it, hone it, direct it, and empower it just as light is directed and made more powerful in a laser. The attention, the directed mind, can be used to reshape, to alter physical reality. That doesn't necessarily take great realization. Tibetans believe it is also possible to alter physical reality by calling on an ally among nonhuman sentient beings.

If you ask whether the experience of primordial awareness exists, the answer is yes. But if you try to objectify, as you are experiencing it, then you can't say that it does or doesn't exist. You can't say both, and you can't say neither. It simply transcends such questions. The question doesn't apply, because the experience transcends anything you can say about it.

When we speak of this primordial awareness, it sounds like something we might one day discover, something that may one day manifest and enter the domain of our experience. At the first Mind and Life Conference, in 1987, the Dalai Lama was asked if our primordial awareness is already present and operating. Is it already manifest in the midst of our day-to-day experience, eating breakfast, going to town, or is that something that is maybe months, years, lifetimes away? A very interesting question.

Before answering, it is worth noting that insofar as this primordial awareness can be articulated, it is said to be self-arisen, utterly spontaneous, effortless, unpremeditated, unfabricated, uncontrived, unconstructed, and the source of all virtue. It's the source of your compassion, your insight, your power. Is this primordial awareness operating and manifest right now?

The Dalai Lama's response was yes, it is. Discovering it is ascertaining something that was always already present, something profoundly familiar—essentially more familiar than anything else could possibly be. It's like coming home. In the same way, recognizing primordial awareness will come as something absolutely fresh and profoundly familiar.

When you achieve *samatha*, they say that you have now "achieved attention." Now you've got it, for the first time. Once you've achieved attention, you use it to explore the nature of reality. And you do this with discernment, with your critical faculties. Now that you have this superb instrument of your attention, you can join this with your intelligence to probe into the nature of reality, the nature of your own identity, the nature of consciousness itself, anything you like. By probing continuously, you begin to transcend attention itself. You go so deep that you leave attention behind. You've transcended knowledge, but you haven't blacked out; you haven't become a nonentity. You have transcended objectification, because by and large, in our usage of the term "knowledge," it's always knowledge *of* something. Here there is no longer knowledge *of*, no longer this or that. There's something that's unmediated, seamless, and you can't say *you* know *it*.

Such realization is a possibility in Madhyamaka practice. The Madhyamaka teachings emphasize objectifying phenomena and penetrating to the emptiness of essential nature. But as you progress in this training, you eventually transcend attention. You may also follow the path of Dzogchen, the Great Perfection. Dzogchen teachings do not so strongly emphasize objectifying phenomena and subjecting them to ontological analysis, but instead emphasize releasing the subjective mind into an unmodified awareness, which is another way of transcending mundane, dualistic attention and consciousness, and releasing into primordial awareness.

It really is very important for us to know that there are people nowadays who have realized this, and I say this with an enormous degree of confidence. There are some very fine masters still living. If we aspire to this, we need have no fear at all that we will come to an impasse because the teachers aren't good enough. The sky's the limit. There are teachers available who can take us all the way to spiritual awakening.

QUESTIONS AND RESPONSES: THE URGENCY AND RARITY OF SPIRITUAL AWAKENING

Question: Given the immense urgency of the many crises facing our global community, is there any way to speed up the process of spiritual maturation?

Response: The speediest way is to conjoin as many conducive circumstances as possible. If you have earnestness but no material support, it can be hard. If you have lots of support, but you're wishy-washy in the practice, it will go slowly. If you have a good environment and great earnestness, but no good teacher, it will take longer. That's what teachers are for: to speed things up. If one were to bring together all the optimal circumstances for spiritual maturation, external and internal, one could really move very rapidly and effectively. It's just harder when you have fewer supporting conditions and more obstacles.

There is no one optimal set of circumstances for everybody, but we can place ourselves in circumstances that are as good as we can possibly bring together. Bear in mind that we are also engaged in the world, and in meaningful activities. Hopefully we're not just biding time or trying to survive. A major component is to make very sure that what you're doing in the world is also part of your spiritual practice, and not just something you have to do in addition.

Then, the practice itself just needs to be implemented. It includes the purification of things like ill will, sensual craving, scatteredness of mind, and so on. It includes attending to the six prerequisites and five barriers to *śamatha*, purifying self-centeredness and all of the far enemies of the Four Immeasurables: ill will, cruelty, revulsion and attraction, cynicism and despair.

Once one has accomplished some degree of stability and vividness, if not *śamatha* itself, it is time to cultivate compassion and loving-kindness, and time to cultivate insight. If we open ourselves up to faith, we open ourselves up to the infinite—once one has accomplished some degree of *śamatha*, *bodhicitta*, and *vipaśyanā*, or insight, then the great shortcut is Vajrayāna. It's said by various traditional teachers that Vajrayāna is not for everybody. The *bodhisattva* path, based on practices such as the cultivation of insight and loving-kindness, traditionally takes three countless eons from the time that you become a *bodhisattva* until you become a *buddha*. It's not eternity, but a very, very long, finite period. This is fine. What's the hurry? If you develop a *bodhisattva*'s insight and loving-kindness, you will have one meaningful lifetime after another, giving service and developing your own virtues. This is an immensely rich spiritual practice, why not savor it? If this sounds satisfactory, then forget about Vajrayāna. You don't need it. Here is a beautiful style of life, from life to life to life, and if it takes three countless eons, well, heck, why not six? Because it just gets better, like a blossom opening up over eon upon eon.

However, you may find that you cannot possibly bear the extent and the depth of suffering in this world. You may be struck with a sense of unbearable urgency, a feeling that it's not enough to be a *bodhisattva*, you've really got to become a *buddha* as fast as possible. The motivation may have nothing to do with your own personal circumstances, as if you could say, "If it's just me, I can take three countless eons, no problem at all. But for the sake of sentient beings, the situation and the environment in which I dwell has become so absolutely urgent, that three countless eons is too long!" If that's the motivation, then you proceed to Vajrayāna, and you can condense three countless eons into one lifetime, or a matter of years. And there are teachers nowadays who can teach it. The Dalai Lama is one, and there are others as well.

A lot of people enter Vajrayāna practice without that motivation at all. They just think: "Oh, the shortcut. I'll take that one. Why take the long way when you can take the short cut?" Or they may find Vajrayāna interesting, or they like a lama who teaches it. There are many kinds of motivations. But if the motivation is not right, you will not attain Buddhahood, or so say the teachers I've studied under. The insight and quality of motivation is essential. Otherwise you are in the wrong program. Vajrayāna is for people who are so unbearably moved by compassion that they must develop towards Buddhahood and bring forth the power and the wisdom and the compassion that enlightenment entails. And of course, you must have some *samādhi*; otherwise you just can't do it.

That's the traditional account of Vajrayāna from very eminent traditional teachers. Other people may say that Vajrayāna is for everybody and they'll invite you right in. Maybe they're right, but that's not what I've heard, and all I can do is report what I've heard from the finest teachers I know.

Question: It's an enigma to me why, in spite of our very essence, the jewel in the lotus that's within each person, the compassion within each person, enlightenment has a poor track record. The statistics are not good. You can name the handful of enlightened beings throughout our recorded history that we have recognized. Maybe there are more, and they don't get as much coverage as bad news does. But why should it be so rare when it's what all religions strive for in their own way?

Response: It may be helpful to focus on the gradient of the path, rather than how many people have reached enlightenment. It's true that a very small proportion of all people have reached enlightenment, but there's a lot of ground between here and there. I'm confident that a significant number of people, far more than we might suspect, have attained deep realization, and it may not be immediately necessary for them to proclaim their insights. It may be appropriate in a certain lifetime to still keep a low profile, to have a direct influence on only a few people.

Most people in the world, including many Buddhists, are frankly not consciously interested in enlightenment. Maybe that will come later, they say. The notion that a human life could be radically transformed in this lifetime, and that the potentials of compassion, insight, and the power of the mind could be unleashed, is not that common. When religions become institutionalized, which is almost invariably the case, the institutions seem to be threatened by that. Jesus made some extraordinary claims about the potential of human life. He challenged us, for instance, to "Be perfect, therefore, as your heavenly Father is perfect."[23] But most Christians have drawn the comfortable conclusion that this is impossible. We identify with and take refuge in our own limitations, thereby concealing our deepest potentials.

Much of the poor track record for enlightenment has to do with environment. The accepted world view suggests that our capacities are extremely limited, and most of science seems to confirm it. The human mind is merely an effulgence of the brain, scientists claim. Christian theology tells us we are instrinsically flawed. Moreover, what change is possible is through grace alone, as if we can do nothing about it. I don't believe this is what Christ said; quite to the contrary. A charitable view of Christian theology would recognize that surrender to the power of God could open the possibility for this radical transformation. A less charitable view would see it as a total disempowerment of human beings. Materialistic science has been equally disempowering. We're being disempowered by the two major sources of authority we have for our whole civilization.

Of course, there are exceptional people who inspire and encourage us to believe that we really do have a profound capacity for transformation and spiritual growth. But they are rare in today's world. You'll find Buddhists who say you can't really change much now: "It's only possible to be a scholar. It's a dark age, and the evil in the world is too strong to do much about it." This issue was brought to the attention of the Dalai Lama by an acquaintance of mine. Twenty years ago, in a private audience, he made this same lament, and the Dalai Lama said that this is nonsense. Is this a degenerate era? Yes, it is. It's a dark time. There is a great deal of evil and distress in the world, and it seems to be accelerating. That's an observable fact. Nevertheless, if one individual should now make suitable efforts, this person has the same chance of bringing about transformation as in a more benevolent era. When it comes right down to the individual, the opportunity is there.

How much of a role does the environment play? We are not just social animals. We may even choose to live in solitude. But we are sentient beings engaged with other beings in this universe. We are influenced by other people's ideas, their judgments, their norms, their values, their lifestyle, their expectations. If we associate closely with people who are committed to the idea that there is very little room for spiritual growth, it will be hard not to be influenced by that. The Buddha declared that half of one's spiritual practice consists of choosing one's companions. This is one of our great freedoms, so let's cherish and take full advantage of it.

Notes

1. Luke 23:34. Holy Bible. New International Version. My references to Christianity during this retreat are certainly not meant to imply that Jesus and Gautama were teaching the same thing. However, I do feel that many of the meditations presented in this book may be practiced effectively and with great benefit by Christians and other non-Buddhists. Many of the ideals and methods here are, I believe, universal in their relevance and value, and I hope they may enrich the lives of spiritual aspirants regardless of their religious beliefs.

2. William James, "The Perception of Reality," in *The Principles of Psychology* (New York: Dover Publications, 1890/1950), p. 322.

3. *A Guide to the Bodhisattva Way of Life*, trans. by Vesna A. Wallace & B. Alan Wallace (Ithaca: Snow Lion, 1997), V: 48-53.

4. Matthew 17:20. Holy Bible, New International Version.

5. These are the concerns of obtaining material acquisitions, stimulus-driven pleasures, praise, and acknowledgment, and the concerns of avoiding their opposites.

6. For an excellent, experience-based account of this approach to *śamatha* practice, see Gen Lamrimpa, *Calming the Mind: Tibetan Buddhist Teachings on Cultivating Meditative Quiescence*, trans. B. Alan Wallace (Ithaca: Snow Lion Publications, 1995).

7. I've discussed this topic and the relation between *śamatha* and *vipassanā* in the Theravāda tradition in *The Bridge of Quiescence: Experiencing Tibetan Buddhist Meditation* (Chicago: Open Court, 1998).

8. See especially his classic work *The Principles of Psychology* (New York: Dover Publications, 1890/1950) and also *Talks to Teachers: On Psychology; and to students on some of Life's Ideals*, Intro. by Paul Woodring (New York: W. W. Norton & Co., 1899/1958).

9. *A Guide to the Bodhisattva Way of Life*, V: 4-5.

10. This is not to be confused with the fourth *jhāna*, or meditative stabilization, described in the Theravāda meditation literature, in which mindfulness is said to be brought to perfection. The fourth attentional state called "close placement" in the Indo-Tibetan Buddhist tradition entails a much more primitive degree of mindfulness than the fourth *jhāna*.

11. See *The Bridge of Quiescence: Experiencing Tibetan Buddhist Meditation*, p. 163, and Karma Chagmé, *A Spacious Path to Freedom: Practical Instructions on the Union of Mahāmudrā and Atiyoga*, with comm. by Gyatrul Rinpoche; trans. by B. Alan Wallace (Ithaca: Snow Lion, 1998), p. 156.

12. For a clear explanation of this practice, see Padmasambhava's *Natural Liberation: Padmasambhava's Teachings on the Six Bardos*, with comm. by Gyatrul Rinpoche; trans. B. Alan Wallace (Boston: Wisdom, 1998), pp. 105-114.

13. *Udāna* 47.

14. This is recorded in *Healing Emotions: Conversations with the Dalai Lama on Mindfulness, Emotions, and Health*, ed. Daniel Goleman (Boston: Shambhala, 1997), pp. 189-196.

15. *A Guide to the Bodhisattva Way of Life*, VI: 10.

16. *The Path of Purification*, trans. Bhikkhu Ñāṇamoli (Kandy: Buddhist Publication Society, 1979), IX: 15.

17. Ibid.

18. *The Path of Purification*, IX: 60-76.

19. *A Guide to the Bodhisattva Way of Life*, VIII: 94.

20. Ibid., VIII: 99.

21. Ibid., X: 55.

22. Ibid., VI: 41.

23. Ibid., V: 3-6.

24. *The Path of Purification*, chs. XII, XIII.

25. Matthew 5:48.